What the
Blind Man Saw

The story of Johnnie Wenger

VELINA SHOWALTER

ISBN: 978-1-949648-95-9

Cover and text layout design: Kristi Yoder

Cover art by Shirley Myers

Illustrations by Igor Kondratyuk

Printed in the USA

Published by:

TGS International
P.O. Box 355
Berlin, Ohio 44610 USA
Phone: 330.893.4828
Fax: 330.893.2305
www.tgsinternational.com

TGS002022

Table of Contents

CHAPTER ONE

Blindness and Broom Making

Michael Wenger watched his son Johnnie pull the pump handle up and down, up and down, as cool water splashed into the bucket. Michael tipped his straw hat with one hand and scratched his forehead as he did when he was thinking deeply. When the bucket was full, Johnnie set it on the ground and waited. He heard his father clear his throat.

"Johnnie, I have been thinking," Papa began. "You said you would like to make brooms. Do you really think you could do something like that without being able to see? Where could you learn how?"

Johnnie lifted his unseeing eyes to Papa's face. "Didn't you hear the discussion the other day at the auction in Blue Ball? Remember the man who was selling brooms and baskets and stuff? He said a blind man made those brooms."

Papa chuckled. "When I am selling livestock I do not pay attention to brooms or baskets. Your ears always hear more than mine. You don't miss much!"

"Papa, I really think that when the fall work is done, and before winter sets in, I want to start making brooms."

"It sounds like you have your mind made up. How about we finish the chores now and talk about it later?"

Johnnie's younger brother Francis had overheard the conversation. He stopped and leaned on his pitchfork as he added his opinion. "Ah," laughed Francis. "Plenty of brooms are for sale all over Lancaster County, including most of the stores in East Earl Township. Where do you think you could sell more brooms?" He flung a bundle of hay into the horses' manger. "By the way," he called over his shoulder, "where would we put up with such a mess?"

Mary stepped out from between the cows, carrying a bucket of frothy milk. "Come on, Francis. If Johnnie thinks broom making is a good idea, let's help him." Mary had a soft spot for her blind brother. "I would think making brooms would be a better project for a man than making baskets."

The conversation was dropped and everyone headed toward the house. The aroma of fried ham and beans floated across the porch of the Pennsylvania farmhouse, and like a magnet it drew the family together at the end of the busy day. The barn chores were completed just as the sun slipped below the horizon. Mama placed a shining kerosene lamp on the middle of the table. The lamplight illuminated their faces as they gathered one by one.

Papa pulled out the chair at the head of the table, and

Mama sat next to him around the corner. Johnnie, as the oldest boy of the family, slipped in at the other end. His brothers, David, Aaron, and Francis, scooted down the bench along the wall behind the table. Lydia, Barbara, and Esther pulled up chairs beside Mama. Lydia hid her shy little face in Mama's shadow, but Barbara sat up straight and frowned at Aaron, who grinned at her from across the table. Next to Barbara, Mary quietly waited with her hands in her lap.

They all turned toward Papa. When Papa bowed his head, instantly everyone did likewise. Reverence and quiet filled the kitchen as their prayers ascended heavenward. When Papa drew in a deep breath to signal the end of the prayer, the stillness was broken by the chatter and clatter of a happy family. The discussion was lively as their plates and stomachs were filled with Mama's good food.

"Mama, did you know Johnnie is going to make brooms?" Aaron blurted, glancing at Johnnie.

Johnnie continued to spoon beans into his mouth as if he had not heard. With a questioning look, Mama turned toward Papa, who was deliberately cutting the ham on his plate. He paused before looking at Aaron. "We don't really know what Johnnie is going to do, but he is thinking about it."

Mama scooped applesauce onto Lydia's plate. "That sounds like a good idea."

Soon everyone had shared their opinions. Johnnie grinned and nodded his head as all the ideas came together.

A few weeks later Papa hitched reliable old Bertie to the light spring wagon. Johnnie and Papa, with little David between them on the seat, headed toward Goodville to meet broom maker Jeremiah Ludwig. Papa had written him a letter, so Jeremiah was expecting them.

David, chattering like a chipmunk, pointed his finger in every direction. He told Johnnie about the beautiful sky, the blue hills in the distance, the green fields, and the valleys. He painted word pictures of the cornfields, the barns, the houses, the farm animals, and the rail fences. The wagon rolled along, over wooden bridges, into the valleys, and up the hills along the curvy country road. It was normal for David to describe all they were seeing because for most of his lifetime, Johnnie had been completely blind.

Johnnie had been born in Lancaster County, Pennsylvania, in 1843. He was still a baby when Papa and Mama realized that their little son could not see out of one eye. School days were difficult for Johnnie because of his limited eyesight. When his school days ended at age fourteen, he was glad to spend more time helping his father on the family farm in East Earl Township.

Johnnie was only twenty-two years old when he lost the sight in his other eye. He was completely blind! It was a hard blow to bear, but gradually he was able to accept that this was God's plan for him, and he learned to face life cheerfully.

"Papa," said Johnnie, who sat erect absorbing all the beauty through David's eyes as they drove along. "I am thankful I could see for so many years before I was totally blind. I remember the things David is describing. It would be much worse if I had been *born* blind! And I am fortunate that I can still smell, hear, touch, and feel."

"It is over twenty years since we discovered you were blind in one eye," said Papa as he steered Bertie into a covered bridge.

"Being blind is probably not the worst handicap," said Johnnie as he put his hand on David's wiggly knee. "I'm glad I have this little brother to tell me all about the things I cannot see."

"Oh, here comes a fine carriage," squealed David as Papa guided old Bertie to the edge of the road. "Johnnie, I see the lamp hanging on the side. It has two seats, and on the back seat are two ladies with fancy hats! They must come from the city."

"I hear the horses have a fancy trot," added Johnnie as the carriage rumbled by.

Entering the village of Goodville, Johnnie heard screen doors banging, children playing in the yards, dogs barking, people walking and talking, and other vehicles on the road. David bounced up and down as he exclaimed about the sights around them in town. Everything was new to David.

When they knocked on the door of Jeremiah's shop, David became quiet.

"Hallo!" boomed Jeremiah. Johnnie decided the man must be partly deaf. The smell of tobacco became stronger as Jeremiah shuffled toward them.

Michael Wenger made polite introductions while Jeremiah added "aha's" to punctuate nearly every sentence. Johnnie hoped he would get busy and make a broom before it was time to go home.

"So," said Jeremiah, "Johnnie, you come here and I will make a broom just for you! You reach out and see with your fingers, but don't let me chop them off with my trimming knife. That would make life unhandy indeed! I hear you have been blind since you were twenty-two years old. That must not be too long ago. I cannot see much since I am old, but I have seen plenty in my lifetime. Aha."

Jeremiah laid an orderly amount of broomcorn out on the worktable. David stuck his nose close to the worktable, and Papa moved closer to watch every move.

Johnnie stretched out his arm, and his deft fingers slipped over the broomcorn laid neatly in bunches on the worktable.

"Now you see," said Jeremiah, "the straw I am using has been soaked in water. I did that before you came so you would not have to wait while it soaked. Sometime I will tell you about growing broomcorn—but not today.

"Now, Johnnie, you be sure and ask questions," the broom maker went on. "That is the way to learn. Can you feel how this treadle is rigged? That's so we can get tension on this wire. The wire passes through three pulleys.

"Aha, that's it. Get underneath the wrapping machine and feel how it works as I pull on this wire. It comes from that spool down there," Jeremiah continued.

"See how I stuck the broom handle into this barrel fastened to the worktable? Now I can work with this end that is exposed. I get my broom handles readymade, but you could make your own if you have a lathe."

"Is this the barrel?" asked David, who was curiously

fingering Jeremiah's equipment.

"Aha, you're right, little David," Jeremiah said. "It's a long hollow pole that looks like a big gun barrel."

"Johnnie knows how to use the lathe. He will mostly make his own handles if I can find the right wood for him," added Michael.

"Aha, you have a fine father, Johnnie," said Jeremiah. "I will show you later where I get all my supplies."

The seasoned broom maker grabbed a bundle of broomcorn from the supply on the worktable. He worked the treadle on the machine as he wrapped wire around the bundle to tie it to the handle. David moved a little closer, and Johnnie had to nearly reach over him to feel the handle, the wire, and the broomcorn. Jeremiah kept repeating this until a nice amount of straw was fastened to the handle. The treadle kept tension on the wire so it was wrapped very tightly.

"Now David, watch your nose, and Johnnie, watch your fingers. Using this sharp knife I will trim the straw neatly around the handle. Aha, that is how it goes.

"Now watch this particular step. You will think I am putting this bunch on backward. I will bend it around to make the shoulder of the broom.

"Now it will fan out like this. Johnnie, come and take hold and feel how it is done."

Johnnie slowly and thoughtfully felt all the broomcorn that was sticking out, ready to be smoothed down to make a neat broom.

"Aha," said Jeremiah, "at this point I will wrap a temporary wire around it right here. Can you feel how I have flattened it? Now we will pull it out of the barrel and go over to the clamp."

"Don't get your finger clamped in with the broom. Feel this. I can clamp it here and here, and that allows me to sew in several places at once."

Johnnie stepped over to the clamp and examined it with his hands.

David looked up at Johnnie. "Hey, this looks like fun work. I hope I can help you sometimes."

Johnnie felt the broom in the clamp. The open end stuck toward the ceiling and the handle pointed to the floor. He felt exactly where the stitches were to be placed while Jeremiah and Michael worked together to cut the string.

"Aha. This will be the hardest part for you. This is where David can help you. You need to thread this string through this needle, and then I will push it through the broom-corn right above the clamp. See, we go back and forth and back and forth, from one side to the other. Use your thumb to measure how far apart to make the stitches so they will be neat and spaced evenly."

Jeremiah settled down to stitch, and this gave Johnnie and Michael time to examine the tools more carefully. Finally Johnnie also put in some stitches. The broom was completed except for the trimming at the bottom. Jeremiah did this with a big pair of scissors, but he explained how some broom makers have a sharp knife attached to the end of the table, and with one whack, they slice off the uneven broomcorn ends.

Johnnie stood for a long time, twirling the broom

thoughtfully in his hands.

"Aha!" said Jeremiah. He was pleased with himself and his finished product. Johnnie could sense the glow on his face.

"What do you think?" asked Papa.

David grabbed the broom and swept it across the floor with all his might. Dust and trimmings flew everywhere.

"Aha, there you go. You have your own shop cleaner right by your side!"

"I think I can do it!" Johnnie exclaimed. He beamed with the prospect of having his own project.

"So how do we pay you for your work today, Mr. Ludwig?" asked Michael.

"Aha, that is my pleasure to do this for you. I know you will be back with more questions. You can bring me a dressed chicken sometime from your farm when you come. I live alone now that my missus is gone, and I do not run to market all the time like she used to.

"Michael, come over here to the light by the window. I will give you the address for a company in New York that sells broommaking supplies. Let me see. Here, I will write it on this envelope: *Orange Judd Company, 245 Broadway, New York.* Of course, many of the supplies you can get closer to home, and you can even make some of the stuff yourself. Johnnie here will figure it out."

Johnnie and Michael both shook hands with Jeremiah. David had already skipped out to see if old Bertie was ready to go home. The sun was low in the sky and they had a long way to go.

All the way home Papa and Johnnie discussed broom

making. David sat between them, his head nodding to the rhythm of Bertie's hoofs on the dirt road. It had been a long day for him.

Johnnie saw the door of opportunity crack open. He was eager to start his own trade.

CHAPTER TWO

Moving to Weaverland

A fierce blizzard swept through East Earl Township early in January 1872. The howling wind entered every crack and piled snow in every corner. Excited children, waiting for the wind to die down so they could go sledding, pressed their noses to the windows and watched snow banks grow to enormous heights. Farmers secured barn doors and kept an eye on their animals in the shelter of the barn. Mothers bent over their cooking pots or relaxed in rocking chairs with their little ones around them.

Johnnie was not in a house or a barn. He was in his own little shop, stitching up a broom and singing a merry tune above the whistle of the wind. Situated by the road on his father's farm, the little broom shop had already attracted a good number of customers, friends, and neighbors. In the corner of the shop sat the first broom Johnnie had ever made, proving his determination and skill. Johnnie's father felt rewarded for his efforts in helping Johnnie build this shop and buying the equipment.

The needle in Johnnie's hand slipped in and out. Suddenly the door burst open and a blast of wind and snow whirled broomcorn in every direction. Johnnie, grabbing what he could, shouted, "Shut the door!"

David and Barbara, gasping for breath, stumbled into the shop and headed for the pot-bellied stove, "Why, Johnnie!" David exclaimed. "The snow is deeper than my boots. You should see those banks! One drift reaches to the barn roof!"

"The temperature is dropping. By tomorrow morning we will have excellent sledding when the wind dies down," added Barbara, rubbing her hands together. "Remember how we used to start on the barn bank and end down by the stream when we were little children?"

Johnnie nodded his head and rearranged the bundles of broomcorn on the table. He added another bunch to the broom he was making. "What time is it?" he asked. "Did you do the chores already? Somehow I lost track of time this afternoon."

Barbara laughed. "Johnnie, someday we will let you work here all night, and you won't even know the difference! We are just on the way to the barn for chores and decided to pop in here first. We must get going."

David sat on a chair. He sighed as he pulled his boot-straps tighter.

"Does your back hurt again, David?" asked Johnnie, noticing his brother's frequent sighs.

"Ah, yes, Johnnie. I don't even want to go sledding anymore."

Dropping his scissors, Johnnie declared, "David, this is no night for you to be out. You go back to the house and Barbara and I will do your chores." After shutting the dampers on the stove, Johnnie and Barbara stepped out the door. The wind snatched their breath and whooshed them to the barn.

Johnnie had no problem finding his way around the old barn. Its peculiar smells and sounds were familiar to him. And unlike the others, he never worried about carrying a lantern. Walking directly into Bertie's stall, he tapped the old mare gently on the rump. "Step over, lady. Are you ready for a drink?" he asked, leading her out to the frozen watering trough. Tonight the ice crust on the water had to be smashed before the horse could suck deep draughts of refreshing water. Johnnie led Bertie back to the stall, and then one by one he led each of the other horses to the trough.

"Hey, Johnnie!" hollered Aaron from the other side of the calf pen. "We need more straw from the straw mow. Why don't you pitch it down since you don't need a lantern?" Without hesitation Johnnie scrambled up the ladder. Soon the straw came plopping down the hole. After all the animals were tended and all the doors shut securely, Johnnie, Barbara, Aaron, and Papa made a dash for the house, gasping for breath and floundering through the drifts.

After supper the Wenger family gathered around the

fireplace in the parlor. A candle flickered on the windowsill, illuminating the dollops of snow on the outside. Barbara gathered her embroidery work into her lap and settled into the rocker by the fire. Mama's knitting needles clicked in rhythm with the clock, while David sat on the hearth with a book spread on his lap. He loved to read to his wiggly little sister Lydia, who pulled her chair up to him, eager to hear another poem or story. David carefully opened the precious new book *Golden Thoughts on Mother, Home, and Heaven.* Lydia stretched her neck and drew her little chair closer. She loved to see the beautiful pictures in the book. Aaron pulled a chair up to Papa and Johnnie and listened to their weighty discussion. Now that Mary and Francis were both married and had their own families, the family circle in the Wenger home was smaller.

Johnnie drew his chair closer to Papa. He leaned forward and in a persuasive voice suggested, "Yes, but I think it would be a good idea to buy the Overholtzer farm in Weaverland. It is such a good location for a business there between Terre Hill and the East Earl Railroad Station."

"I must say," added Papa, "it probably would be a good place for you with this broom business sweeping you off your feet." They all chuckled at Papa's little joke. "I know you need more space. I did hear there was a store in the Overholtzer farmhouse at one time."

Mama laid her knitting in her lap and stared into the fire. Then she hesitantly added her voice to the conversation. "But this is where we brought up our family and started housekeeping."

"And I like going to school here in the winter," added David, shoving his book aside.

"Ah," added Aaron, "you know enough. You read all the time and nobody in East Earl Union School will miss you."

Papa looked sharply at Aaron. "So, shall we say nobody will miss *you* at the gathering at Reidenbach's Store on Saturday evening?"

Barbara's face glowed in the flickering firelight. "I would love to live in Weaverland!" she exclaimed. "I already have some friends there."

Lydia, the youngest in the family, had nothing to say.

Papa looked intently at Johnnie. He shifted his legs and took a deep breath before speaking. "But Johnnie, my concern is you. How will you find your way around? Here you know where all the doors are, the hay-holes, the ladders, the gates, as well as the lanes and the fences on the farm. You go through all this without difficulty. How would it go for you at a new place?"

Johnnie smiled and tilted his chin up and gazed toward the ceiling. "I like challenges," he replied modestly. "I envision a store and a business for David and me. I don't think you need to worry about how I would manage."

The family batted ideas back and forth until the wind died down and the fire in the fireplace flickered lower and lower. One by one they slipped off to bed. Papa tossed and turned under the feather tick until the old mantel clock struck twelve. *I will do it all for Johnnie,* he thought, and then sleep overtook him.

By the time spring promised another growing season, the business transaction was completed. The Isaac Overholtzer farm in Weaverland was now the possession of Michael Wenger. Moving was planned for the month of March.

March came like a lamb. Snow banks vanished and little rivulets of water trickled across the meadow and gurgled down the stream. Dandelions pushed fuzzy, yellow blooms out of the soft spring grass. But in the Wenger home, moving took priority and the dandelions bloomed unnoticed.

Mama wrapped the glass bowls and plates in her linens and packed them carefully into the wooden barrel Papa had rolled into the kitchen. "Esther, you put all these spoons into this chest. Barbara! Don't worry so much about what Aaron might be doing out by the barn. Let's get all this stuff ready to go by tomorrow morning. Lydia, you can put these crocks into this crate." Mama kept everything organized as she issued orders left and right.

While the women worked in the house, Aaron gathered the tools from the shop and ran here and there wherever Papa ordered him to go.

David and Johnnie worked like a team in the broom shop. "Are you sure you want this bundle of broomcorn out on the wagon?" wondered David as he gathered another armful.

"Yes, sir!" exclaimed Johnnie. "Let's get this shop stuff loaded before supper." Carefully he laid all his tools into a wooden crate he had made especially for this occasion.

"David!" Johnnie exclaimed. "I have big visions for the future. You know I want to have a real store with more than just brooms. You would make a good clerk, and together we will run a business."

By the time the sun went down, the Wenger farm no longer looked like the orderly home it had always been. Johnnie bumped into obstacles on his way to the kitchen for supper, but he did not mind. The excitement of moving and the anticipation of a new home with better opportunities was worth any trouble that came with it.

Aunt Magdalena met him at the kitchen door with a kettle of soup in one hand and a dipper in the other. Her cheerful voice rang through the house. "Come and eat your soup while it's hot. I have a stack of bowls on the kitchen table and some spoons in a basket." Aunt Magdalena always made Johnnie feel warm inside. He knew she was smiling and her big heart had room for everybody.

Mama pulled a handkerchief from her pocket and dabbed tears from her eyes. Softly she whispered, "I hate to leave behind the graveyard on the hill. Dear little Samuel and Magdalena—I liked to walk up the hill and lay wildflowers on their graves." Memories of the day when she watched Baby Samuel's tiny coffin being lowered into the grave flooded her mind. She remembered little Magdalena, so pale and sickly, leaving this world at the tender age of three.

For a moment all was silent as everyone glanced around the old familiar home, now in disarray. Then Johnnie spoke up. "Weaverland is not that far away," he said cheerfully.

"Remember our forefathers moved all the way across the ocean and left much behind! At least we can come back and see what's happening to the old home place."

The next day the sun was peeping over the horizon as the Wengers pulled out the familiar farm lane, their wagons nearly overflowing. They turned up the road toward Weaverland. Papa came first, his spring wagon loaded high with furniture and household items. The two brown work horses followed, pulling a wagonload of odds and ends. Nobody expected them to go very fast, even though Uncle Henry was the driver and he usually pushed things to the limit. But speed was not important today.

Aaron drove the next team of horses. He drove the wagon filled with Johnnie's broom making equipment, and Johnnie and David rode with him. In the last rig of the caravan, Mama rode with the girls in the buggy, pulled by Bertie, their favorite horse. Bertie traveled much slower now than she had the day she trotted to Goodville with Papa, David, and Johnnie to meet old Mr. Ludwig, the broom maker.

"Hold your hats!" called David as the March wind grabbed his hat and rolled it into the meadow. Aaron quickly reined in his horse, hopped from the wagon, and dashed after the spinning hat. The wind played havoc all day with the moving caravan. Canvases that covered the furniture flapped noisily and made the horses edgy, but on and on they plodded until the sun was high in the sky. Then one by one the wagons pulled up to the new home.

David slowly climbed from the wagon. His back ached but he was anxious to show Johnnie all around the place.

"Here," he said as he opened the gate, "is the door to the barn. Follow me and I will show you the cow stable and the horse stalls." Johnnie did not hesitate but walked along, carefully noting the new layout.

After they had explored the barn, Johnnie and David walked across the road to the stone farmhouse. However, they soon felt they were in the way as many people bustled about finding a place for everything. They decided to explore the house later.

The brothers walked down the curve in the road toward the river. David pointed to the trees and told Johnnie all about his new surroundings. "Here we come to the bridge," he explained. "On the other side is the sawmill and the flour mill." When they came back to the house, it was neat and orderly and ready for the Wenger family.

Time went by and soon Johnnie had mastered the new place. He found his way around the buildings as well as the fields. When he was out in the fields and the dinner bell rang, he headed back across the fields, climbed the fences, and came out at the gate behind the barn every time.

Papa looked at Johnnie as he came in the kitchen door. "Johnnie," he said, "I think I will get lost in this place before you do. Remember how I worried about you getting around? The saying is true: Half the things we worry about never happen!"

Johnnie realized how pleased his father was with the new place in Weaverland. He felt confident that it was a good move.

CHAPTER THREE

The New Shop and Store

On a fine summer morning, David gently guided the horse round and round to turn the power sweep. With its gearbox and a shaft, the sweep turned a circular saw for Johnnie. One broom handle after another was laid aside, cut to the exact length.

After the broom handles were cut, Johnnie took them into the shop. There he used his foot to spin the lathe, his deft hands gliding over the wood until each broom handle was just the right thickness, round and smooth. *Just perfect,* he thought as he laid another handle on the pile.

Johnnie's mind also circled round and round while he worked. *If I could get a gasoline engine from the New Holland Machine Company, I would no longer need the power sweep! The horse could be used on the farm and I could do this by myself!*

David walked into the shop and sat on a barrel to rest. Johnnie, suspecting it was David, heard him sigh as he sat down. He recognized the footsteps of the family, just as other people recognized faces. "David," he began with enthusiasm, "the next time I go to New Holland, I want to buy a gasoline engine. You won't believe what all I will be able to do with it. We can get rid of that power sweep because the engine can turn the saw. And I can fix it up so it will pump water too!"

Sometime later Johnnie walked the country road to New Holland. After a stop at the bank, he walked to the New Holland Machine Company building. Johnnie's mechanical mind buzzed with ideas, and he enjoyed a lively discussion with the workers. He had to get his hands on all the machines. Before he left New Holland, he had ordered his engine.

Several weeks later, under the shelter of a little house by the well, a gasoline engine puttered. Not only did the engine connect to the saw and lathe, but it also pumped water for the livestock on the Wenger farm. Johnnie's ideas had become reality, and the power sweep sat unused by the barn.

Papa entered Johnnie's shop and pulled a chair closer to the potbellied stove. "Winter is coming to Weaverland in a hurry," he drawled as he rubbed his cold hands together. Johnnie continued to shove the needle through the thick broom, stretching as he pulled the string through the other side. Back and forth, back and forth, Johnnie worked the needle across the broom.

"I've been thinking," began Johnnie as he tied the knots to hold the thread in place.

"I don't doubt that," interrupted Papa dryly. "I can't keep up with your ideas. What am I to expect next?"

"I've been thinking," started Johnnie again, "that I would like to build a new shop and a small store. I have not forgotten the store idea. You know David will never manage with the farm work. His crooked back hurts him so."

Papa nodded. "I know you need more space. But can you and David handle more changes and more work?"

"I have the plans all in my head, and I'll get David to draw it out so you can see what I have in mind."

Papa sat up straight. Johnnie was a step ahead again!

David pulled a chair up to the little table in the corner by the window but said nothing. Elbows resting on the table, he rested his chin in his palms.

"Johnnie, are you sure you can build a store?" questioned Papa. "It takes more than just drawing up the plans. By spring, Aaron and I will have lots of farm work. The fences need to be repaired, and of course there is always the seeding and cultivating."

Johnnie knew what spring on the farm was like. Before Papa could add more to the list, he said, "Yes, I know. But David and I can do it. I'll order the lumber soon, and when spring comes we'll be ready to start. George, that bachelor across the fields, said he could help me build."

Papa stepped toward the door. "Well, I won't stand in the way. You can go ahead and we will see what happens."

When the door closed, Johnnie pulled a crate up beside David. "Do you have a pencil?" he asked. "We can start on the plans right now!"

David rolled his eyes in disbelief, but he soon had a paper and pencil ready. Carefully he wrote down every detail as Johnnie dictated the plans. Obviously Johnnie had spent a lot of time planning it all. It did not take long for David to get it down on paper.

A few days later Johnnie said to David. "Come with me. Let's go down to the sawmill and order the lumber for the new shop!"

Johnnie strode along the road and over the bridge. Johnnie's confidence often caused David to forget that his brother was blind. The owner of the mill came out to meet them. Pulling a pencil from behind his ear, he scratched the details onto a piece of paper as Johnnie explained what they needed.

The water flowing through the mill race slowly turned the water wheel beside the mill, but the whine of the saw drowned out the sound of splashing water. The saw blade moved up and down, and Johnnie listened carefully as the log slowly moved along. How he wished he could get his hands on all those pulleys, gears, and belts—when not in use, of course! Waterpower fascinated him.

"Now, Johnnie," said the sawyer, "all you need is some horses and a wagon, and we can get the lumber where you need it. Or are you going to carry it home piece by piece? We never know what you might do next!"

"We will have a wagon here when you are ready,"

assured Johnnie.

A few days later Johnnie walked to Wechter's Store in Terre Hill to buy the nails and other hardware he needed.

"Hello, Johnnie!" Mr. Wechter called from behind the counter. "What are you up to now?"

"We are going to build a new shop and store out there on our farm," explained Johnnie.

While Mr. Wechter weighed out the nails and screws, Johnnie wandered to the porch where a group of neighbors chatted and laughed as they exchanged tidbits of news.

Old Mr. Long, tilting his chair and stretching his suspenders with his thumbs, sucked in his breath to catch the attention of the crowd. "Have you all heard about the trouble with the Indians in South Dakota?"

"Nope," snapped Little Joe, "but if it has anything to do with Indians, I know it is trouble."

"Don't jump to conclusions," objected Tall Tim. "The government is trying to work things out properly. They offered the Lakota Indians $25,000 for land out there in the Black Hills. They asked the Indians to move onto reserved Indian Territory."

"And do you know what Chief Spotted Tail said?" asked Wise Willy. " 'If it is such good land, send the white man there and let us alone. We were not born on the reservation and want nothing to do with it.' "

"You're right, Lakota resentment is growing," added Mr. Long. "It hasn't been that many years since the Fort Laramie Treaty gave the Indians all of western South Dakota—forever."

"Another problem we have to face is running the Northern Pacific Railroad through the great buffalo hunting grounds," someone added.

"And a railroad we must have!" shouted Little Joe. "Custer is out there, and he sent a telegraph across the nation saying that gold has been discovered in the Black Hills."

"And who is Custer?" wondered a customer who was striding up the steps and caught the drift of the conversation.

Johnnie, sitting on a keg, shuffled his feet and cleared his throat. All eyes turned to him. "I do not understand what happened with that Custer fellow, but his roots are right here in Pennsylvania. The Custers are a Mennonite family from the old Skippack congregation in Montgomery County."

"Just think of it!" exclaimed Wise Willy. "Now he is Lieutenant Colonel George Armstrong Custer on an army expedition exploring the Black Hills with 110 wagons and about 12,000 men!"

"Believe me," added Little Joe, nodding emphatically. "In these hard times many more will head out west hoping to pan gold."

Catching up with news from near and far was important to Johnnie. He walked away, shaking his head and sympathizing with the Indians out in South Dakota.

Before Johnnie left town, he stopped at Davis & Watt's General Store and bought a copy of *The Terre Hill Times*. He would ask David to read it to him that evening.

As soon as winter was past, while the farmers cultivated

their fields and planted their crops, Johnnie started on the building project. The ring of hammers pounding and the rasp of saws cutting boards sounded through the valley. Neighbor George loved to build, and he and Johnnie worked as a team to raise the walls for the new store and broom making shop. By the time the farmers were ready to cut hay, Johnnie was ready to organize his new store.

Papa stepped into the new store. He grinned with satisfaction as his eyes roved from wall to wall and from floor to ceiling. *It happened again,* he thought. *Johnnie gets ideas, makes the plans, and gets it accomplished!*

Johnnie made many business trips. He walked three miles to catch the train that puffed its way into the cities of Philadelphia and Lancaster. Crates of supplies were ordered and delivered to the store and shop. The news spread around the community that Johnnie's new store was open for business.

The big day arrived. One lovely morning in June, David opened the store and stood behind the counter, waiting for customers. With a satisfied feeling he looked at the kitchen supplies on the shelves on one side; the baskets that hung from the ceiling; the boxes of crackers; the bins of flour, oatmeal, and cornmeal along the side wall; the candy in little compartments on the counter; and the big burlap bag of peanuts on the floor in one corner. Of course, a wide wooden barrel with brooms standing on their handles stood right inside the door.

Just then a buggy rattled up to the hitching post. Joel King, their jolly, old neighbor, stepped into the store and

looked around. "Well, you don't say. You already got your store filled up!" He grinned broadly. "I'll have two pounds of those," he said, pointing his crooked finger at the large bag of peanuts.

Carefully David scooped up the peanuts and plopped them onto the scales. Tipping the pan, he poured the peanuts into a brown paper bag, pulled some string off a spool, and wrapped the string around the bag. He tied a knot and handed the package to Joel, exchanging it for a dime. The first business transaction in the new store was complete!

Like bees in a field of clover, the neighbors buzzed around Johnnie's store. One day Johnnie heard the heavy steps of Gertrude Stauffer come into the store. *Tap, tap.* Her full skirt rustled as she walked up to the counter. "Johnnie," she said in a high-pitched voice, "I will need two pounds of cornmeal, three pounds of oatmeal, and oh, I see you have lots of eggs. My hens quit laying and I would like to bake a cake. So I will take a dozen eggs."

Johnnie carefully dipped the cornmeal onto the scales. He filled a bag, then reached for another bag to hold the oatmeal. He scraped the oatmeal from the barrel and muttered something about the barrel being nearly empty. A salesman had just walked in the door. "Johnnie, I guess you would give a good bit to have your eyesight restored," he commented as he watched Johnnie work.

Johnnie wrapped the string around the bag and tied a knot. "Not as much as people might think!" he quipped. He counted the eggs as he placed them into Gertrude's basket. "Is that all for you?" he asked cheerily.

"Well, I think I need one of those caramels. I always did have a sweet tooth," Gertrude confessed. So Johnnie reached under the glass and carefully laid a caramel into the basket.

"The cornmeal is five cents, the oatmeal ten cents, the eggs are now thirty cents a dozen, and the candy is one cent. So your total is forty-six cents."

Carefully Gertrude laid a penny, a nickel, and four dimes on the counter. Johnnie picked up the coins and inconspicuously felt their edges. Then he dropped them into the right compartments in the cash box. Gertrude *tap, tapped* out the door, and Johnnie discussed some issues with the salesman. Business was brisk in the Wengers' store.

When the young folks gathered on Saturday afternoon, Johnnie and David enjoyed listening to the stories and latest ideas from the whole neighborhood. The store became an active meeting place, and this gave Johnnie another idea.

"David," he said, "why don't you and I make ice cream for all these fellows who hang around on Saturdays?"

David jerked as if ice had hit him. *What will Johnnie come up with next?* he wondered.

Johnnie grinned. "I have it all figured out. You just wait and see. I will get an ice cream maker the next time I go to Lancaster, and we will learn how to do it! Just think of how much everyone would enjoy it!"

David fidgeted on the stool he was perched on behind the counter. Puckering his brow, he stammered, "Johnnie . . . where would you . . . get the supplies?"

"Oh, that's not a problem. The cows here on the farm

give us plenty of milk, and that Jersey has rich cream. We already have the sugar and salt in the store, and the chickens supply us with eggs. And sister Barbara has the best recipe for it!" Johnnie had it all figured out again.

"But the ice? Where do we get ice in the summertime when cold ice cream is a real treat?" ventured David.

"People have ice saved in ice houses. I know where I can get some and it is right close by."

Johnnie continued with his plans and David stood by, eager to see what would happen next. They had a new store. They had a new shop. Business was picking up and Johnnie continued to "see" many ways to make it flourish.

CHAPTER FOUR

The Wheelbarrow and New Ideas

In the broom shop Johnnie carefully arranged the soggy broomcorn on the workbench. His fingers swiftly glided over the broomcorn and neatly placed it around another broom handle. He twisted the wire tightly. Then he called to David, who was in the store. No customers were there at the moment, and the door between the shop and the store stood open. "David, come here. I want to ask you something."

David came to the doorway, and for a quiet moment his thoughts rambled while he watched his blind brother work. *So much has happened since that day we went to Goodville to learn how to make brooms.*

Dear sister Esther died soon after that. Thoughts about

Esther's illness and death made him brush a tear aside. *I was only seventeen when she died. No one else cared for me with as much compassion as she did. Maybe it was because she was never strong and robust like the rest that she could relate to my handicap of a crooked back. Aaron is already married for eight years. It looks like Barbara and Lydia will always stay at home.* His thoughts were interrupted as Johnnie called to him a second time.

"Hey, brother, where are you?" asked Johnnie. David's startled chuckle made Johnnie laugh. Johnnie seldom missed noticing that someone was nearby. "Are you ready to make ice cream again on Saturday, which I guess is tomorrow already?"

"I guess," said David, mentally calculating what ingredients he needed.

"Those boys really seem to enjoy it. Why don't we make several batches this week? There is still plenty of ice stored in that old lime kiln. I will help you bring it over in the morning, but you can get the rest of the ingredients together this afternoon as you have time. Check with the girls to see how much cream is on hand."

Early in the morning David was in the back of the store stirring the mixture to make ice cream. He had done it so many times he no longer checked the recipe. Johnnie had brought a big hand-crank ice cream freezer home from Lancaster. Usually David did the mixing and Johnnie did the churning. Together they went for ice.

The neighbor men had cut the ice blocks during the winter. After the blocks were cut from a nearby pond, they hauled them by sleighs to an abandoned lime kiln. Part of the old stone kiln lay underground, and the men had to stoop to enter the low doorway. They packed the ice blocks in layers of sawdust brought by the wagonload from the sawmill across the road. Many of the neighbors used this ice to keep food cold in their iceboxes during the summer.

"David, where is the basket I use to carry ice?" called Johnnie as he entered the store.

"Oh, it is sitting in the wheelbarrow ready to go," called David over his shoulder. "I will be ready in a few minutes."

But Johnnie did not want to wait a few minutes. He had already walked across the road and was on the footpath that led to the wide Conestoga Creek where a huge log spanned the water and served as a bridge. Johnnie carefully walked across the log, never lifting his feet very high, but sliding them along the log. Soon David came behind him with the wheelbarrow. Together they piled the slippery ice blocks onto the wheelbarrow using some strong tongs. Then Johnnie filled his basket. With careful steps, they crossed the log again and returned to the shop.

Johnnie put the ice into a bag, and with a hammer he crushed it fine. "This will make a nice batch," said Johnnie to himself, "but I think we will need some more today."

David was busy with customers in the store, so Johnnie opted to go by himself. *I cannot carry enough in my basket, so I will take the wheelbarrow,* he reasoned. He had no problem finding his way. He pulled the wheelbarrow across the log, feeling satisfied with his accomplishment. Loading it with ice was not a problem. Because of David's back problem,

Johnnie was used to doing the heaviest part of the work. He loaded the wheelbarrow extra full and grabbed the handles. He was just ready to head back across the log when he heard Papa call urgently, "Johnnie, stop!"

Johnnie dropped the handles of the wheelbarrow and listened to the running footsteps approaching. "Johnnie," reprimanded Papa, "don't ever try to do something so dangerous again!" Johnnie sighed and let Papa take over the load while he followed. Of course, Johnnie did use the wheelbarrow again, and eventually Papa learned to trust him. Johnnie took the wheelbarrow to the trolley station and hauled freight back to the store. And he dared to take many more trips across that log with the wheelbarrow.

The ice cream seemed to turn out exceptionally good that hot August day.

||||||||||||||||||||||||||||||||||||||||||||||

Another Saturday afternoon, the neighborhood boys loafing around the store were in a jolly mood. "Johnnie, where is your wheelbarrow?" hollered Pete. Johnnie emerged from the store at that moment. He walked behind the store and pulled the wheelbarrow out for them.

"Now what are you up to?" questioned Johnnie.

"We are having a contest," replied Joe, who was a natural ringleader. "Look, everyone. This is what we will do. Bob, you pound this stake into the middle of the meadow." He pointed behind the store. "See, here is a wheelbarrow," he continued. "I will blindfold each of you—one at a time—then we will take turns and see if you can hit that stake with the wheelbarrow."

Johnnie calmly said, "Show me where the stake is."

So his nephew, Willie, said, "Follow me." He knew how to lead his blind uncle by the hand. Johnnie grinned as he walked back to the crowd and stood in the background to see what was going to happen.

Whoop-pee! Everyone shouted. This should be easy! They clapped their hands and pranced in circles like school boys.

"Now calm down and line up," ordered Joe as he tied a bandana over Henry's eyes. Henry grabbed the wheelbarrow and crazily spun out into the pasture, missing the stake by a long shot. The whole group roared with laughter until he was frustrated and whipped off the bandana.

Henry tossed the bandana into the wheelbarrow and pushed it back to Toby, who stood about a foot taller than the rest. "Hey, get me a ladder," Joe teased. But he managed to tie the bandana around Toby's eyes without one. Toby took long strides and passed the stake as he continued down through the pasture. The other boys started yelling, and he knew he was off track. He ripped off the bandana and without a word wheeled the wheelbarrow up to Slim Sam.

Sam quietly tied his own bandana and carefully stepped out across the meadow and headed straight for the Conestoga Creek. "Stop!" the onlookers shouted. They doubled over, hooting with laughter. Poor Sam untied the knot and came back.

Then Joe himself tied on the bandana and confidently strode across the meadow with the empty wheelbarrow bouncing in front of him. He whipped around in a circle realizing he was making a fool of himself. Subdued, he brought the wheelbarrow up to Johnnie and said, "We'll have you try it."

Johnnie, who was as old as some of the boys' fathers, was still up for some good fun. Joe tied the bandana over Johnnie's eyes. Johnnie pretended it was not adjusted right and pulled on it to make it fit. He grabbed the wheelbarrow and headed straight for the stake. Jerry, one of the younger boys, yelled above the din, "Johnnie, you are peeking!"

Wham! The wheelbarrow hit the stake squarely!

The boys cheered and clapped loudly enough for the whole neighborhood to hear. Johnnie pulled the wheelbarrow back, and the boys slapped him on his back and congratulated him as the winner.

The boys were still talking about it the next day after church.

One day, Johnnie's sister Lydia heard a clatter outside the farmhouse and hurried to the window to see what was going on. To her surprise, Johnnie lay in the dust, and the wheelbarrow was tipped on its side beside him. She gasped in horror. *That certainly doesn't happen very often,* she thought.

"Barbara!" Lydia called. "Johnnie just fell over the

wheelbarrow. I see him getting up." She watched him for a while before she said, "He seems to be all right."

Johnnie, brushing the dust from his face, heard a mischievous little snicker close by. Ignoring it, he finished his chores and went to the store where David was still sorting mail. He helped several customers before he went to the shop for the rest of the day.

A week later Johnnie was tending the store when he heard the door open. He knew someone had entered and was lingering near the entrance. Without hesitation, Johnnie marched out from behind the counter. His big hand clamped down suddenly on the shoulder of the culprit, and then Johnnie gave the boy the sound whipping he deserved. Taken completely by surprise, the boy whimpered, "I, I, am sor-sorry." He slunk out the door muttering, "I will never trip him again. How did Johnnie know it was me?"

|||||||||||||||||||||||||||||||||||||||||

"Papa, do you know what I heard yesterday in New Holland?" asked Johnnie as he scooped the last of the cherry pie from his plate.

Papa shoved his empty plate back and turned toward Johnnie, anticipating another new idea.

Mama, who was carrying a stack of dishes, stopped in her tracks between the table and the sink. Barbara paid no attention and dipped hot water out of the boiler on the stove into her dishpan. David pulled his chair closer to Johnnie. What would they hear now?

With a grin Johnnie continued, "I learned about the hay tedder."

"A what?" questioned Papa.

"A hay tedder. It turns the hay for you so the sun can dry it more easily."

"Now, Johnnie, don't try to make me believe a machine is needed to do such an easy thing. Even before our fore-fathers stepped onto American soil, pitchforks have been used to turn hay!"

"But, Papa, think of all the time you would save. You could have bigger fields and fewer people to work for you."

"Well, tell me how it works."

The rattle of the dishes quieted as the girls stopped to listen. Mama returned to her chair at the table. "Johnnie," she said, adding her two cents to the conversation, "we can be satisfied with the old ways. I hear of so many new things. Aunt Betsy told me she heard about a gadget called a camera that can make a picture of somebody. And that is not all—I heard somebody is foolish enough to think that someday a machine will run down the road instead of our horses and carriages! "

"Of course," said Johnnie. "Those ideas about horseless carriages are real, and after a while we will see it happen! Machines will do most of the work we do now by hand. But right now I want to tell Papa more about this hay tedder because I think he should have one!"

Now Johnnie had everyone's attention as he continued, his fingers motioning as fast as the words tumbled out. "This is how the machine works—the main frame of the tedder is bolted together with angle brackets. The tedder has forks made of spring steel that kick up and down as the machine is pulled through the field by horses. A chain drive turns sprocket wheels that are connected to the main crankshaft, then sprockets and chains dispense the cog gearing. There is a simple shifting device located within the reach of the driver, so the height of the forks can be controlled by a lever. You hitch one or two horses to the tedder and pull it across the windrows and watch the hay fly!"

"Ah, I still don't see how this is going to work," said Papa doubtfully.

David stroked his chin thoughtfully. "Johnnie, how did you figure all that out?"

Johnnie shoved his chair back from the table and tilted it on its back legs. He rocked gently back and forth, totally captivated with the idea of a new machine. "My fingers told me how it works, and my ears heard how it runs."

Papa was still trying to think through all this when Johnnie exclaimed, "Hey, Papa, here is the deal. I will order one and put it together. Then you can try it out for yourself." Papa agreed and walked away smiling.

The following week Johnnie got down to some serious business. The tedder was delivered from the train station to the shop in a big wooden crate. Papa had gone with his team of horses and wagon to pick it up, and he watched eagerly as Johnnie pried the crate open.

M-mm, this will be a puzzle, admitted Johnnie to himself, but aloud he spoke confidently, "I am ready to tackle it tonight. I have studied the tedder on display in New Holland, and I am sure I know how it should go together."

So that evening when the farmers had retired from their field work and David had locked the store for the night, Johnnie carefully pulled all the pieces from the crate and laid them in order on his shop floor. In the darkness he turned the nuts and bolts into place. He felt each chain, each sprocket, each cog gearing, and pondered how it should function. He worked the gears with his hands until he was satisfied they were correctly in place. Slipping the wheels into the axles, he adjusted the seat and then fastened the pole, the double tree, and the neck yoke. He pulled the assembled tedder carefully out of the shop and slipped into bed just as a new day broke over the eastern horizon.

When Papa came out to the shop, he could hardly believe his eyes. There, right in front of him stood the new machine, ready to run that very day! Johnnie came out and slipped his hands once more over the machine. Then he was ready to let his father try it.

Papa hitched two horses to the tedder and drove to the field. Johnnie followed the machine and listened carefully as Papa slipped it into gear. He heard the happy *clacking* as the tedder kicked over the half-dried hay. What a satisfied feeling it was for Johnnie to know that he had put it all together the way it was supposed to be!

Papa made a round, and Johnnie sensed that Papa was very happy indeed. "Johnnie!" he exclaimed, "this machine is doing an excellent job! I think I shall buy it from you, and we can show the other farmers what a tedder can do!"

Johnnie saw how a piece of equipment could indeed help a farmer. He was ready to assemble other new machines that would make farming more efficient.

CHAPTER FIVE

The Binder Business Begins

The newspaper rustled and Johnnie pulled a chair closer to David. Evenings were the time for them to relax. "What is interesting in the paper today?" asked Johnnie. "Anything new?"

David did not reply immediately, then he chuckled. "Listen to this episode. 'Mrs. John Hess in Pleasant Grove was going upstairs in her home and came into contact with a large black snake coiled on the window. The snake measured five feet in length.' I am sure she had a scare!"

"That is not of any significance to me," answered Johnnie. "Who cares how many ladies have snakes in their houses!"

"Well, here it says the Cherokee Indians are dying

rapidly. They are considered civilized but they still depend on medicine men for their cures. They live in Osage—wherever that is."

"It is in Oklahoma," Johnnie said. "I think it is a pity that those Indians are pushed out of their land like they are. I cannot understand why there wasn't a fair way to deal with the natives of this country," he added sadly. "Is there any news about Custer?"

"Yes, actually there is. The paper claims Custer shot a grizzly bear—on August 7, 1874, to be exact—and he says this was his greatest achievement as a hunter."

Johnnie changed the subject. "What are the prices of wheat and oats?"

"Well, wheat is eighty cents, oats forty-three, and corn is sixty cents a bushel just now."

"Those are good prices, and soon the wheat harvest will begin. I am excited about that!

"David," Johnnie continued, "lay that paper down and listen to this. I heard that tomorrow near Martindale they are demonstrating a self-tying binder. That is really going to change how we farm!"

David laid the paper on an empty chair and shuffled his feet. "But," he began timidly, "How can that be? If a binder ties the sheaves, many people will no longer have work."

Papa walked into the house and pulled up a chair. He scanned his sons' faces, wondering what the conversation might be about now. Johnnie continued, "Papa, did you know that tomorrow I am going to watch the demonstration of a self-tying binder?"

"Times are changing," sighed Papa. "I remember well how we used to cut wheat when I was still a boy at home. We used only a sickle or a grain hook."

"Yes," added David, "then you had to stop and sharpen your sickle. That must have been annoying."

"No, no, it was not annoying—it was just part of it," explained Papa. "Some things took extra time. We fastened a stump iron to our waist with a strip of leather. Then when the sickle was no longer sharp, we stopped and pounded the stump iron into a fence post or stump. We hammered the blade against the iron, using a special scythe hammer until it was sharp again. It took skill but once you learned how to do it, it made the work easier."

"David, I remember those days. You were a baby when we first saw the mechanical reaper," said Johnnie.

"Papa, remember the day the horses almost lost their heads when we hitched them to that sail-reaper?"

"Oh yes, those rotating paddles behind them really spooked the horses at first. But the sail-reaper was a real change in wheat harvesting. After that we had a McCormick reaper with a sheaf-tying platform. A man had to stand on the platform and rake off the bundles. Johnnie, you remember that one, don't you?"

"Most certainly," Johnnie said. "I always preferred raking off the wheat rather than tying the sheaves. It took some skill to push off just the right amount so the women did not complain about the size of the bundle."

"I am satisfied with what I have today," Papa said.

"But Papa, just think," David said. "If we would have a

self-tying binder nobody would have to ride on the platform to tie the sheaves." Then he sighed. "I guess it doesn't really make much difference to me how you do it, because I am not able to help with the harvest anyway."

"It would go so much faster if the sheaves would plop out of the binder tied and ready to set up in shocks!" Johnny insisted. "These self-tying binders are popping up all over the country. Papa, you have seen them. And I will see to it that you get one."

"Oh, we shall see," answered Papa. "One invention follows another. Some are good but others are not very practical. One man never has a chance to try everything."

"Just think of it," added Johnnie. "Farmers can plant bigger fields and harvest more grain with fewer people."

Johnnie jumped to his feet and stretched to his full height. "Now, tomorrow I want to see more demonstrations using the self-tying binder!" he exclaimed.

"So, you already have your plans made," said Papa. "I thought I could tell *you* about it! Why don't we both go? David can keep the store and I will take you over."

Early the next morning Papa and Johnnie arrived at the wheat field near Martindale. Farmers in bib overalls, straw hats, and boots milled about joking and laughing. Papa looked left and right and drawled, "There are more farmers here than wheat stalks in the field."

All day long farmers in buggies, wagons, or carts rumbled up and down the dusty road. Some trotted in on horseback and tied their horses to the rail fence. It seemed somebody was always coming or going.

"Move over!" hollered a farmer coming with a fresh team of work horses. It was time to change the horses on the binder doing the demonstration. The driver brought the machine to a halt while the men changed horses.

Johnnie, full of questions, stood in the circle with the farmers talking to the dealer. "And what is this gear doing?" he asked, slipping quick fingers over the mechanism. For a long time he fingered the knotter. He listened carefully as the machine clacked in rhythm when the hand crank turned the gears. His thumb slipped over a tied sheaf that spilled out from under the canvas. His hands followed the twine to the spool. At just the right moment, the knotter twisted the twine together and tied a sheaf securely. Johnnie grinned with satisfaction. The function of the knotter clicked in his mind and he "saw" how it worked.

Johnnie walked around and listened to the discussions. "You know," said one farmer, "I thought I had the latest when I got a McCormick reaper that cut the grain and raked it together on a canvas before it dropped it to the ground."

"Yeah, but that still makes a lot of work. Tying sheaves is what takes the time."

"Many farmers are still happy with the grain cradle." The grain cradle was an invention that cut crops at a uniform level.

"I wonder if such a machine will put inventor Joe Shirk out of business?" wondered another farmer as he watched the binder go clacking around the perimeter of the patch of grain still standing in the middle of the field.

Johnnie chuckled to himself as still another farmer

drawled, "We don't need the latest inventions. God said a man is to work by the sweat of his brow to make a living. That binder will make it too easy for the farmers."

"But see," added another spectator, "this binder cuts the grain and ties the sheaves! There has never been anything like it before. Just think what this will mean! More work done—more money in your pocket."

Johnnie, ready to tackle a new machine, had his mind made up at the end of the day. He knew he would be able to sell binders.

|||||||||||||||||||||||||||||||||||||||||

This decision in the early 1880s changed Blind Johnnie's world. After several trips to Philadelphia and Lancaster and a visit from the dealer of the Johnston Harvester Company in Batavia, New York, Johnnie had his binders coming. As time passed, he added more and more farm implements to the list of equipment he assembled and sold.

"We could have a post office in our store," declared Johnnie one day as Papa came in with some mail. Papa laid the letters on the table and opened his mouth as if he wanted to say something. But before a word escaped, Johnnie went on. "We could be a branch of the Terre Hill post office, and the people in this community could pick up their mail here. Or they could bring mail here to send out. Mail goes daily to Lancaster, Cedar Lane, Reading, and Ephrata on the rails."

"The next time I go to town for the mail, I will see what

we can arrange," Papa agreed.

David was listening in. "Are you sure you want to add more to the store business? We are busy as it is."

Johnnie clapped his hands together and without hesitation exclaimed, *"Ach*, David, we can do it. It will bring all the more people around!"

David wrung his hands and sighed. He looked outside the store where a customer was tying his horse to the hitching post. *And why do we need more people? The implement business takes up Johnnie's time, and I am busy enough as it is.*

David's thoughts rolled in circles, until they were interrupted by the customer waiting at the counter. "So you have a number of implements ready to go?" the man asked. "I saw another hay tedder out there and a mowing machine. The farmers have so much modern machinery nowadays. Can you imagine what our grandfathers would think if they would see it all?"

David, carefully weighing out the cornmeal, had enough to do without worrying what the grandfathers would think. He went right on with his business.

Before that customer left, neighbor Sally Sue came into the store and bustled up to the counter.

"I want to trade this butter for eggs," explained Sally, digging in her basket. "My hens are not laying like they should. I am suspicious they have a hidden nest." Johnnie picked up the butter and paused. He felt the lump of butter carefully several times. Then he twisted it. Sally glanced at him furtively, shuffled her feet, and wrinkled her brow. Then she declared more loudly than necessary, "I just made that butter yesterday and kept it in the crock in the spring. I make the best butter because we have a Jersey cow."

Johnnie patted the butter and said, "Something seems different." Sally's eyes opened wide and her mouth dropped as Johnnie reached for a knife. With one *whack!* he exposed a sweet potato hidden in the butter! He grinned broadly, packaged the whole mess with brown paper, and shoved it back to Sally.

Sally gulped as if she could have swallowed her tongue and slunk out the door.

Johnnie and David laughed until the tears rolled!

Then Johnnie said in a more serious tone, "I must get busy. I need to unpack the crates that arrived from Batavia, New York. The binders have come and I want to assemble one tonight for Moses Weaver."

The sun went down but it made no difference to Johnnie. He kept right on working even after the rest of the family had gone to bed. All the parts were laid out in an organized way, and Johnnie carefully bolted pieces together until a binder took shape. He ran his hands over the gears and listened for the proper click of the cogs. He tightened chains and greased axles. After he had stretched out the canvas, he fastened the seat. Finally, he attached the tongue and pulled the complete machine from the shop.

With a satisfied feeling, he crawled into bed when the roosters were crowing.

When Moses Weaver arrived, Johnnie was up again and

out beside the machine, ready to demonstrate how it operated.

Moses examined every detail while Johnnie explained carefully how it worked. "You will need twine to put into this bin. I have some for sale in the shop." He hurried to the shop and soon came out with a big spool of twine and plopped it into the bin. Moses watched every move as Johnnie threaded the knotter. "There, now you are good to go!"

"I'll leave my wagon here and hitch the team to the binder," Moses said. "The wheat field is not too far from here. Neighbor Noah is out with the grain cradle opening up the field."

"I'll be there to give you more instructions when you are ready to start," Johnnie said as he began walking toward the field.

An hour later, Moses was all ready to go. Johnnie stood back, out of the way. Noah had cleared the path around the edge of the field, and the horses, twitching nervously, waited for the command to go. Moses perched on the seat as delighted as a child with a new toy. "Gitty-up," he said as he tapped the horses gently with the line in his hand. The binder began to cheerfully clatter along. Everything worked just fine!

Johnnie walked behind the binder and listened carefully to the mechanics of the machine. One sheaf of wheat after another plopped out onto the stubble. Two men tried to keep up with the shocking. As the sheaves dropped to the ground, the boys snatched them up with pitchforks and arranged five or six sheaves of wheat in a cluster, propping the heads up against each other to make shocks. All morning long they worked in the field. The binder ran smoothly, and soon it was far ahead of the boys.

Later in the day Johnnie walked home feeling satisfied indeed. This was just the beginning of a busy season, and more and more farmers came and ordered binders. And Johnnie made sure Papa was on the list too.

One day later that month Johnnie walked out to the barn where Papa and the neighbors were getting ready to bring in their second crop of hay. "How's it going?" he asked the cluster of men on the barn bridge.[1]

"We are having our share of problems," confessed Noah.

"But how is it going with you?" interrupted Joel. "I hear you have a binder running for Moses."

"It is going well," replied Johnnie modestly. "The sheaves are rolling out—tied snug and tight. The boys can't keep up!"

"Someday we will all have binders like that," said Henry. "But before I get a binder I want a tedder like Michael here has. That sure works slick."

"Did you see the dump rake work?" asked Joel. "That Johnston machinery has the competition beat."

"Hey, do you want to be my salesman?" asked Johnnie, slapping him on his back. "Did you know I can get you a hay loader too? I'm going to demonstrate a Johnston mower down at Samuel Sauder's soon."

"You don't say? I want to be there for that. By next year

---

[1] A barn bridge is the wooden or dirt ramp up to the second story of a barn.

I want to have my own mower," added Henry, the young farmer who had been married just the week before.

Everyone stepped back. Two horses pulling a load of hay and guided by ten-year-old Amos slowly came up the lane and headed straight for the barn. Amos parked the wagon right under the big fork that dangled from the ropes and pulleys hanging from the track high up in the peak of the barn.

Another horse was hitched to the rope, and the fork plunged into the hay. The horse stepped forward after the first command. But something was wrong. Everybody shouted, "Whoa!" Young Amos pulled on the reins and the old horse halted immediately. He knew when it was an urgent command.

"Something is not lifting right!" shouted Sam from the wagon. Papa scrambled from the hay mow and all eyes shifted to the empty fork dangling above the wagon.

Johnnie had his hands on the rope. He tugged on it a bit before he said, "You men do not have the pulleys and rope hung right!"

Everyone listened as Blind Johnnie explained how to fix the problem. And it all made sense. Noah scrambled to the peak inside the barn, readjusted the pulleys, and got things moving again. Henry said, "And to think that a blind man had to tell us!"

Johnnie chuckled. "I would rather be blind than dumb!" he quipped.

Everyone laughed. Nobody could say it like their good old friend Johnnie Wenger!

CHAPTER SIX

Binder Troubles

David slipped the mail from the bag and placed it into the proper boxes. He straightened his back the best he could and watched Johnnie enter the store with another box of merchandise. "Johnnie," David began, "we are getting too crowded in this store and your implement shed is over-flowing. We need a bigger place."

Johnnie stopped in his tracks. He could hardly believe David would suggest the idea. He himself had been toying with a brainstorm for a long time. "Well, you are part of the business, so you absolutely can share your opinions. You know I officially registered our trade name as *J. S. Wenger & Bro.*

"We will definitely have to come up with some more

space somewhere. Here, carry these nails out to the shop. I did not realize they were in this box of stuff."

The screen door slammed and Johnnie listened to see who was there. In a high-pitched, screechy, female voice, someone said, "I want Ike Horst's mail." Johnnie puckered his brow and reached for the mail in the little compartment. He handed a letter over. Then in a normal voice a fellow laughed, "No, I came for Joe Weaver's mail." Johnnie did not like to be fooled. He snapped, "You get out of here! Why don't you talk sensibly anyway?" Johnnie turned to David and they both chuckled.

A few mornings later when David turned the key in the lock and opened the door of the store for the day, he looked around suspiciously. *Something feels amiss,* he thought. *I did not know I left some brooms on the floor last night! And what is this?* A filthy glove was lying on the counter. Then he noticed the bins of flour and sugar tipped open. Items had been knocked from the pegs on the ceiling, leaving some empty gaps. "Johnnie, come quickly!" he called. Johnnie dropped his tools and marched to the store. What was going on?

"Johnnie," David said anxiously, "somebody was in here last night. The sugar and flour bins are hanging open, some things from the ceiling are missing, and look here! The cash box is empty!"

"How can this be? Is there any evidence where they came in?"

David looked at the window and noticed it was open a crack. He realized how easy it was for thieves to slide it up and crawl in. "Now, who would have the nerve to do this?" he wondered.

"I guess we will never know. We can suspect it was the blacks from Welsh Run, but I don't like to put that blame on them. There are some tramps in Terre Hill that I wouldn't trust either." Johnnie sighed.

"We had only a few dollars in the box," said David, reaching for the glove and heading for the woodstove. "I will soon have things in order again."

"If they need the stuff, they may have it. But I would rather give it to them than have them steal it," declared Johnnie. He left for the shop where he had more projects going.

Kneeling by an unassembled mower, he heard a horse and buggy coming into the drive at a rapid pace. John Eby's buggy skidded around the corner, a cloud of dust billowing behind it. The horse stopped abruptly outside the shop. Johnnie brushed the dust from his knees as he rose to meet the man.

"Johnnie, I have a lot of wheat to harvest and I fear it will rain tomorrow. The knotter on my binder is giving us a fit! The knots are loose and when the sheaf rolls out the wheat scatters. The men who are shocking the wheat are so frustrated."

"Aha," responded Johnnie as he listened to John's troubles. *Seems to me like* you *are frustrated,* thought Johnnie. "I'll hop into the buggy, and we will go over and take a look." Before Johnnie had his feet completely in the buggy box, the wheels started rolling.

John Eby continued his story as they rode along. "We pulled the binder in beside the wagon shed because it is too hot to do repairs in the sun. My father and I have been trying to find the problem, and we have wasted a whole hour!"

"Over here is the binder." John motioned with a full swing of his arm as they clattered into the farm lane. Johnnie followed John to the binder and spoke to the men gathered around. "Turn the crank that brings the machine into motion."

There was a rattle and a clatter as the machine swung into gear. Johnnie listened for a minute or so. "Stop," he indicated with his hand. When all was quiet again, Johnnie said, "Take the knotter apart. You will find a shaft in there the size of a lead pencil. I think it is bent. Straighten the shaft and then I will help you reassemble the knotter." The men followed Johnnie's instructions carefully. The crank was turned again and to everybody's relief the knotter ran smoothly. The horses had been resting during this time, and they were ready to pull the binder out to the field. Now the sheaves fell out tied snugly and securely. The boys who were shocking the wheat had caught up, and everybody was ready to get back to work.

Johnnie drank a dipperful of refreshing lemonade offered to him. Then Grandpa Eby took him back to his shop.

"You know tomorrow will be the demonstration at the Sauder farm," announced Johnnie at the supper table.

"And what is to happen there?" wondered Mama. She could not keep up with all that her blind son was doing.

"*Ach*," said David, "Johnnie wants to show what his Johnston mower can do."

Johnnie did not want to leave the impression that he was boasting or showing off. So he explained, "This is something that the farmers *want* to see. Different dealers come and we all like to compare what different makes can do."

Papa added, "It usually turns out to be an interesting time even for those who are not buying anything."

| | | | | | | | | | | | | | | | | | | | | | | | | | | | | | | | | | | | | | | | | | |

Samuel Sauder anxiously prepared for the show. *This timothy grass is just the right height for a nice test plot,* he decided.

"Just look at this!" shouted Simon Harris, the dealer for the McCormick reaper, as he entered the field the next morning. "This young grass is perfect for a test plot." Simon glanced over at Johnnie who stood beside his Johnston reaper. Throngs of farmers milled around the edge of the field, casting curious looks at the mowing machines. Schoolboys perched in the branches of the trees in the fence rows and balanced on the split rail fences. Laughter rippled across the crowd, serious buyers discussed their options, and stylish businessmen with notebooks in their hands mingled with the throng. The air was charged with expectancy.

Prancing horses, polished for the occasion, parted the crowd as they were brought into the field for a mower demonstration. All eyes turned to the teams and, like a lull before the storm, everyone watched as the first mower

clattered down through the field and left a swath of *uncut* grass behind it. The desperate driver halted the machine. The crowd swarmed around him like buzzing bees. Some squatted on the ground while others plopped on all fours. They looked, they felt, they scrutinized the machine from every angle, until the demonstrator motioned for all to step back, and he made one more attempt. But this young timothy grass was fine and slippery, making it difficult for his machine to cut. He had to give up and pull off to the side to make way for the next demonstrator.

The McCormick dealer was next. Simon handled his fine team of Belgians with ease. He sat erect on the seat, and his grin broadened as his sickle bar slithered through the slippery grass and left a clean shave behind. With a whoop and a holler farmers followed, waving their hats. They nodded their heads as they assessed the situation. This was a success!

Now one more machine had to show what it could do. The crowd tensed as they watched a team of black Percherons march to the Johnston machine. A whisper rippled through the crowd. *This is Blind Johnnie's machine.* Johnnie stood back with his hands in his pockets and his face turned upward, not missing a beat. His fashionable driver confidently commanded the horses. They lifted their big feet with ease and plodded almost gracefully down the field as the throng moved along. The mower cut another clean swath before it circled back to the starting point.

Now the farmers' tongues were all in motion. Heads bobbed up and down, and the men pushed back their hats and repositioned them as if to clear any fog from their brains. Decisions had to be made.

Ladies brought buckets of lemonade to the field, and thirsty men and boys dipped into the buckets and slurped down gallons of the free drinks provided by the implement companies.

The sun rose in the sky and the heat of the day shriveled the freshly-cut grass. Many farmers dwindled away and followed their own pursuits, but Johnnie was surrounded by a crowd that had many questions. He led some curious farmers to the cut grass and knelt on the stubble. With a swoop of his hand, he explained to Samuel Sauder, "Yes, the Johnston mower cut an inch shorter than the McCormick."

"That's it!" Samuel exclaimed as he clapped his hands. "You have sold another mowing machine!" So the transaction was made.

Johnnie's implement business increased, and another big shop was built to accommodate the business.

Later in the summer during wheat harvest, Mr. Huntley from the Johnston Harvester Company visited the community. The Pennsylvania farmers were pleased to meet this man, despite his fashionable clothes and notebook.

Moses Weaver was having some trouble with his binder. "Let's get the factory man to see if he can find the problem," suggested Moses to his son Henry.

"Sure," Henry replied, "I would like to meet the man anyway, and this is a good excuse."

Moses added, "I heard he is staying in the Fairville Hotel

in Terre Hill. Why don't you go over in the morning and offer him a ride out to our farm."

The next morning Mr. Huntley enjoyed his ride out to the Mennonite farm country. When he arrived at the wheat field, he laid his notebook down beside the binder and squatted down on the stubble. He fiddled with the mechanism on the binder. He tried this, and he tried that, while sweat rolled from his brow and dripped off his nose.

Moses tipped his hat back on his forehead and pulled his watch from his pocket. He paced around the binder like a lion in a cage. He looked anxiously at the position of the sun in the sky and then at his binder that was not running.

Moses looked at Henry and said in a quiet tone, "Go fetch Blind Johnnie."

When Johnnie came, he stood beside the binder and listened carefully to the mechanism as Mr. Huntley turned the crank. He asked Moses to pull forward a few yards and then he said, "Whoa!"

Johnnie crawled underneath the binder. There in the stubble, flat on his back, he reached up and made the necessary adjustments. After that the binder purred along perfectly. Poor Mr. Huntley's red face turned redder. *It is good that Johnnie cannot see Mr. Huntley's expression,* thought Henry. Mr. Huntley thanked Johnnie for coming out and promised he would see him again soon.

Several evenings later when Johnnie pulled the door of his shop shut, he heard a buggy drive in. *Surely not another customer this time of the day,* he thought. But it was. Jake from East Earl stepped out of the buggy. "Hello, Johnnie, how is business?"

Johnnie recognized the crackly voice and modestly replied, "Pretty good, Jake."

Then Jake rambled right on into his troubles. "I bought another farm and we have thirty acres of wheat to harvest. My son Ben is using my binder on his farm and we need another binder right now! Do you have any more available? I really want it tomorrow!"

Johnnie hesitated, scraping the toe of his shoe in the gravel. He slowly replied, "I have already sold fourteen this season and I have only one left. But it is not assembled."

"Oh, but couldn't you get it together for me?" pleaded the anxious farmer.

"Well, I suppose I could have it ready to go by morning."

"I knew you would do it!" said Jake.

As the buggy rattled out of sight, Johnnie walked slowly back to the shop and opened the door. He wheeled the wooden crates to the middle of the shop with his bag truck. He pried the lids open and laid all the parts out in order. The night was quiet and he hummed a tune as he worked, fastening the tongue to the finished implement as morning broke. He had slept for only an hour before the anxious farmer came up the road with his wagon and team of horses.

"Sure enough, Johnnie, I knew you could do it!" exclaimed the happy farmer. "I will use it today!" The farmer did not notice Johnnie's weary look or slow steps. Johnnie gratefully accepted the cash that was offered. He was satisfied when his customers were satisfied. Whistling a tune on his way to the house for breakfast, he heard the wagon and binder rumble across the bridge and up the road. *There goes binder number fifteen. That is enough for this summer,* thought Johnnie.

CHAPTER SEVEN

A Bigger Store and Broomshop

Autumn colored the leaves and another harvest season came to a close. Johnnie and David sat down to draw the plans for a new two-story house to be built on land they had bought from Papa in 1886, just across the road from the big stone farmhouse.

"Let's build a section at the back for a broom shop," suggested Johnnie. David's pencil scratched on the tablet as the plans took shape. "The store will be in this part," said Johnnie, motioning with his hands.

David's vision grew as he watched the plans on paper take shape. "That is a good idea to sleep in the upstairs. Maybe we can hear if thieves come in."

Before frost locked up the land, the carpenters came

and laid the foundation for the two-story house. The walls were soon up and the roof was on as well. Now the snow could come. All winter long David and Johnnie worked inside the new house as they had time. Occasionally others came to help them.

When spring came, there was a big moving day from the little store and post office to the new house. David finally had all the space he needed. He watched willing friends and neighbors carry things to the new store.

"I will arrange the broom shop all by myself," said Johnnie as more help arrived. "Then I will know where everything is. David can supervise the moving in the store and the post office."

David carefully organized the store, and Johnnie came in and fingered it all until he knew his way around again. Johnnie had a picture in his mind of all that was spread out before him in this new store.

Finally the two brothers, little hump-backed David and strong Blind Johnnie, settled into their new bedrooms above the store to experience the sweet sleep of laboring men.

"Daniel, would you like to go with me to John Brubaker's funeral in Rohrerstown?" asked Johnnie when his nephew walked into the shop. "You know he was a veterinary and a preacher."

"Johnnie, I do not know all the people you do," said Daniel with a chuckle. "I am not a traveler like you, and going to funerals is not what I do for a hobby. But because you are my uncle, I'll go with you."

So the following day Johnnie and Daniel were swallowed up in the crowd at the old Mennonite meetinghouse. This funeral was of great interest to Papa and Mama, though they were too old to join the crowd themselves. The next morning when Johnnie stepped into their kitchen, they had many questions.

"Who preached in the home?" asked Papa, pulling his chair up beside Johnnie's. He was getting hard of hearing and wanted to hear the whole story.

"A.D. Wenger preached at the home service first, and then again at the meetinghouse where I was," explained Johnnie. "I was told that a thousand people were at the meetinghouse!"

"How could they all fit in?" interrupted Mama.

"They didn't all fit. Many crowded on the porch. And while one service was held at the meetinghouse, C.M. Brackbill preached to another group of a thousand people who filled the schoolhouse."

"This must have been a record-breaker indeed!"

"But wait till you hear this. I was told that another crowd of people gathered on the porch of Barbara Souder's house and the crowd spilled out onto the Marietta Pike."

Papa and Mama shook their heads and sucked in their breath in a deep sigh.

"I suppose the surrounding fields were full of horses and carriages," commented Papa. He tried to envision the huge gathering.

"And how did young Daniel manage to find the way over there?" worried Mama.

"Mama, you know I could easily find my way to Rohrerstown," Johnnie said quietly.

"*Ach,* Johnnie, I know you have a keen sense of direction. I can trust you, but I do wonder sometimes how you manage."

"Well, Mama, I cannot exactly explain how it happens. Sometimes my nose helps me. I can always tell when I am close to Terre Hill because I smell the tobacco factories. I may not be able to see, but God gave me the other four senses for a reason."

Johnnie rose and stepped toward the open door. "Well, Mama and Papa, I would like to visit longer, but Henry Weaver is threshing, and I want to go over and see how it is going." He grabbed his straw hat and ran down the porch steps.

As he walked to the Weaver farm, his mind was busy planning and thinking of new inventions others were developing. His thoughts were interrupted by the roar of an engine, the throb of the belt, and the whirr of the threshing machine. In his mind he could see all the gears and pulleys. He smelled the fresh straw being blown onto a pile. His heart beat with excitement. Times had changed in his day. Machines could now do work in a day that once would have taken ten men a week to accomplish!

He stood near the machine and absorbed it all. He had just pulled his hankie from his pocket to blow the dust from his nose when Henry walked up to him.

"Hey, Johnnie, what do you think of all this?" asked the excited farmer.

Johnnie grinned and nodded. "This is a dream come true. Farmers are leaving the grain cradles, flails, and pitchforks in the dust!"

"Not the pitchforks!" corrected Henry. "Abe is busy on the wagon feeding the sheaves into the machine. Those teeth are gobbling them up in a hurry!"

Johnnie shouted above the noise of the machine, "I'll help fork the sheaves in!"

"But Johnnie! Are you sure?" gasped Henry. Without replying, Johnnie climbed the ladder, grabbed a fork, and began to pitch sheaves into the massive machine.

The man on the wagon dropped his fork and stared, but he let Johnnie join him. The mechanic tending the engine stopped in his tracks and watched Johnnie fork sheaves. The farmer minding the machine raised both hands in surprise. The ladies in the kitchen, with their hands in the dishwater, gasped in alarm and then clapped their hands over their mouths. The boy carrying the water pail to the thirsty men pointed to the wagon, where Blind Johnnie kept pitching sheaves until the wagon was empty.

Johnnie stood beside the threshing machine for a long time, enjoying the rhythm of the mechanism deep in the belly of the machine. He wisely refrained from running his fingers over the moving parts. Slowly he turned and walked back to his own shop, feeling satisfied that he had been allowed to help feed that powerful threshing machine.

||||||||||||||||||||||||||||||||||||||||||||||

Johnnie's sisters Barbara and Lydia still lived in the farmhouse, caring for their aging parents and keeping house for the hired man. David and Johnnie ate their meals with them as well. Poor Barbara was also blind by this time, and Johnnie tried to comfort her in her distress.

"Johnnie," she pleaded when he came in for supper, "could you please bring in some milk from the springhouse? Lydia went to a quilting and is not home yet, but I tried to make the meal."

"Oh, Barbara, you know we are here to help you in any way possible."

Hurrying to the springhouse, he came back with a pitcher full of milk. Then he pulled a chair up to the stove. A cold autumn wind whistled around the windows. David came in and pulled his chair up to the table, anticipating supper. He realized the meal was not ready yet because Lydia was not at home. He glanced around the kitchen and wondered what he should do to help.

While they waited, Johnnie helped everyone to relax. "Let me tell you a funny story," he started. "This past summer, on the very last Saturday we made ice cream for the crowd, I took my cane to walk across the log to the ice house on the other side of the creek. I usually don't use a cane, but I do think it is better to use it as a guide when I cross that log. Anyway, as I slid my cane along the edge, someone grabbed it."

Barbara gasped, and David said, "Oh, no!"

"Do you know what I said right away? I just said, *'Now, Jerry!'* and he let go of the cane immediately."

"How did you know it was Jerry?" wondered Barbara.

"That is just what Jerry wondered," said Johnnie. "I told him nobody else would be as mischievous as he is!"

They all laughed. They all knew Jerry, the neighbor boy.

Just then the door opened and Lydia breezed in. "Is supper ready?" she asked as she pulled off her shawl and slipped off her bonnet, hanging them on the hook behind the stove. "I did not mean to come home so late, but Betsy's horse doesn't go much faster than I can walk, and we started off later than I hoped we would." She bustled to the stove to stir the potatoes. "Oh good, Barbara, you nearly have it ready!"

"Why, nobody even bothered lighting the lamp. The sun is slipping down already and it is so dreary in here," she said with a chuckle. "I guess we could save oil and eat in the dark!"

They all pulled their chairs around the table and waited while Henry, the quiet hired man, joined them. Everything about Henry was too big. A huge nose and enormous ears added character to the man wearing extra-large overalls. But underneath it all was a big heart, and Henry was much appreciated. Slipping onto the bench behind the table, Henry bowed his head for silent prayer before the evening meal with the Wengers.

After the prayer Lydia broke the silence. "Johnnie, are you making brooms these days?"

"Yep, since the weather is colder and the harvest is over,

I like to stoke the old potbellied stove and make brooms. I find the work relaxing."

"Well, after supper some cousins from Maryland want to stop by," said Lydia. "They are visiting in the area for a few days. They don't have much time, but they would like to see you in action—if you are making brooms when they come, that is."

So after supper Johnnie busied himself in the shop until he heard a knock on the door. "Come in," he offered warmly. "So you are the cousins from Maryland?"

After the formal introductions and the traditional hand-shaking, Johnnie said, "Follow me. I have a project going by the workbench. I cannot possibly make a whole broom in this short time, but I am ready to put this into the clamp."

He rattled his tools and everyone stayed quiet until he heard a snicker. Puzzled, Johnnie asked, "Is something wrong?" The cousins burst out laughing.

"Well," Mary, the oldest in the group, said, "we cannot see! It is dark!"

Johnnie joined the laughter and reached for the lamp. "I am sorry," he said. "I just forgot. When the birds stop singing, I know it is time to light the lamp!"

CHAPTER EIGHT

Trips, Trolleys, and a Telephone

"Harry, would you like to go with me on a trip to Lancaster next Wednesday?" asked Johnnie. His nephew Harry had just walked into the store for the mail.

"Most certainly. That would be an adventure!" answered Harry without hesitation.

"Well, you go home and ask your mama and papa, and if I don't hear anything different I will plan on it. And by the way—we will walk the three miles to Blue Ball early in the morning and catch the train into Lancaster."

Johnnie could not see the grin on Harry's face and the sparkle in his eyes, but he heard his nephew dash out of the store faster than usual.

The next Wednesday morning Harry arrived very early,

wearing a freshly ironed shirt and a pair of new trousers. A few coins jingled in his pocket. The sun peeped over the horizon just in time to watch Harry and Johnnie start on their walk to Blue Ball.

As they walked along, Johnnie said, "You know, this network of railroads across the country certainly makes traveling a lot easier."

"Do you remember when they used stagecoaches?" Harry asked.

"Indeed yes. Some coaches are still running today, but these trains are shoving them into the background. Imagine—it takes a train only five hours to get to Philadelphia."

As they trudged along, Johnnie's mind turned back to the days when coaches took passengers from Lancaster to Philadelphia. "You know," he said, "my father, who was your grandfather, used to tell the story how he went to Philadelphia on a four-horse stagecoach. He paid three dollars and boarded the coach at the Fountain Inn on South Queen Street, and by the next evening he was in Philadelphia. They say there were sixty-two taverns along the King's Highway between here and Philadelphia. Just think!"

"And what did they need that many taverns for?" wondered Harry, kicking a pebble along.

"The horses needed to be fed and rested. Often they would trade teams and start out fresh, and people needed to refresh themselves too. Of course the taverns were there for the Conestoga wagons also."

"Tell me about them, Uncle Johnnie."

"In my father's time it was not unusual for a hundred huge wagons to pass through Lancaster in a single day. The main road to the west went through Lancaster. Imagine the clatter of six great horses, the jingling of bells, and the shouting of drivers. Steam trains have mostly replaced the wagons in our day."

"I think I would have liked to be a stagecoach driver rather than a wagon driver. It looks more like a wild and exciting ride!"

"It would not have been so exciting if robbers would have held you up, or if you would have met another wagon or coach when the road was too narrow to pass."

"What would they do when that happened?"

"Sometimes they had to take wagons apart and sometimes they would get stuck in the mire."

"But believe me, new things are coming. Henry Ford is working on an automobile. Before long machines will carry people all over the place."

"Yep! If I ever marry and take my family to church, I will spin along in an automobile and all the horses and carriages will be left in the dust," Harry declared.

"You do have big ideas! Don't we turn right here to get into Blue Ball? I can already hear and smell the cattle yards. They must have a drove of cattle ready to move west."

Harry could no longer walk calmly. Horses were tied to the rail, and the buyers and sellers shouted, protested, and bragged about their beasts. Harry's excitement made him jump and clap with the rest of the gang. "Stay close to me," Johnnie encouraged. "Don't wander away and

get lost in the crowd. After all, we came here to catch the train. Not to buy a horse."

They continued their walk to the train station and bought tickets to Lancaster, and when the train pulled up they climbed on. Harry held his breath and leaned back on the seat as the train rolled along. This was a new adventure—moving down the tracks without a horse! "Uncle Johnnie," he hollered, "I see fields of cows and sheep gliding by. Oh! There is a horse rearing up at the crossing. He does not like the train. And over there, children are waving at us. Do you think they are jealous that all these people get a chance to ride the train?"

As they entered Lancaster, Johnnie said, "Our first stop is at the bank. It is at the corner of East King and South Duke Streets, right beside Miller's Hotel. After we have been to the bank, I will take you to the market."

Harry paid no attention to the plans. His nose was pressed against the window. He watched the ladies on the sidewalk with their market baskets, the men in fancy coats and hats, the horses and wagons of many shapes and sizes jamming the street, and the clusters of people visiting in front of shops open for business. This was not at all like what he was used to in the country.

Harry's mind was already on to the next thing. "I see the jail! I know it is the jail because Papa told me it has a round watchtower over one hundred feet high. Uncle Johnnie, I wish you could see the gateway, those narrow windows, and the high walls. I wonder what it looks like inside."

"I hope you never find out," commented Johnnie. "The

next time the train stops, we will get off."

Johnnie walked straight to the bank and took some time doing business there. Harry's eyes darted from the tall windows to the high tin ceiling with its fancy designs. He followed Johnnie to a few other places of business. As he walked, he read the signs out loud. "Fulton Hall, Demuth Tobacco Shop, Red Lion Inn, The Cat Tavern, The Plough Tavern, Lancaster Journal Printing, and there is the Trinity Church with its high steeple."

"Do you see the statues of Matthew, Mark, Luke, and John at the base of the steeple? That is one thing I remember my father pointing out to me when I came to Lancaster with him as a little boy." Johnnie's voice trailed off with the memory. They walked another block down the street, then Johnnie said, "Isn't this a restaurant here?"

Harry stopped in his tracks and right there in front of him was the sign: "Country House—We serve the best food in Lancaster."

"This is where we will get our noon meal before we go home," said Johnnie.

"Yes, Uncle, but how did you know it was right here?"

Johnnie chuckled and said, "Well, back there is a gutter in the pavement to carry the spouting water from the roof across the pavement, and I knew the restaurant door was so many steps beyond that."

"Oh," gasped Harry in disbelief. "You mean you have to count steps as you walk?"

Harry glanced around the dim dining area. *I think maybe Mama's kitchen might have better food,* he thought. He walked quietly beside Johnnie who pulled out a chair from the table.

"And what can we get for you?" asked a crisp voice. "Today we have chicken served with mashed potatoes, gravy, and peas, or you can have liver with onions and a baked potato and corn. *I hope he chooses the chicken,* thought Harry, but at that moment his tongue stuck to the roof of his mouth and he had nothing to say. He heard Johnnie say, "Two chicken dinners, please."

Harry enjoyed the meal and decided it was as good as Mama's after all.

After dinner they walked to the farmers' market in the square before they headed home. Many vendors were already cleaning up for the day, but Harry had much to say and see. "There are so many carriages and horses tied to the hitching posts! Lots of Mennonites are loading up their wagons. Oh, that lady has an armful of bread left over. Hey, that man has chickens in a tub that is too heavy for him to carry. I see lots and lots of cheese. I wonder if they have *Koch Käse*[1] like my mother makes. Uncle Johnnie, I see Cousin Fannie over there. She is folding up her quilts." Harry chattered on and on, while Johnnie visited with people and took in the sounds and smells peculiar to a market.

Then they found their way back to the train station, and as the sun was setting they trudged into their own lane again. Harry waved a big goodbye to his uncle and

---

[1] Koch Käse, literally, "cook cheese," a spreadable cheese.

shouted, "Thank you!" as he hopped into his papa's buggy. Johnnie had enjoyed seeing Lancaster through the eyes of a boy.

Spring turned to summer, summer to fall, and fall to winter before it was spring again. This cycle promised many fruitful seasons for the farmers in Lancaster County. Summers kept Johnnie busy with the implement sales. Fall brought the joy of harvesting.

Johnnie always enjoyed roaming around the farm to *see* how the crops were growing and how the corn ripened. Taking an ear of corn into his palms, he examined it carefully before walking to the hay field where he slipped the tender blades through his fingers. In the wheat field he rubbed the kernels of wheat between his fingers to determine their ripeness. Johnnie loved the farm he now owned. His parents had passed away in 1900.

Johnnie always had work in the shop assembling or repairing implements, but he also spent time with David in the store.

One morning Johnnie asked David. "Do you know what I heard the other day in town?"

David was putting new dishes on the shelf. "Johnnie," he said, "I do not hear half the things you do, and I don't go half the places you go."

"The Conestoga Traction Company built a trolley line to Blue Ball in 1904, but can you believe this?" Johnnie went on. "Now they are extending it to Terre Hill. To think they used to pull trolleys with horses. Now electricity is common, so they switched to electric cars."

David kept on pulling dishes out of the barrel of sawdust. "Where will the new trolley station be?" he asked while he brushed a dish carefully with a clean rag. He gave the plate on the shelf a little nudge to set it in the proper angle.

"It will be just up the road past the Weaverland Roller Mill, if what I hear is true."

"My, that will be handy indeed! Then I won't see you at home anymore."

"Nah, David, it won't take me away more—but it *will* be so much handier."

The two brothers worked side by side all morning in the store. Johnnie enjoyed hanging around the store, meeting customers and listening to tales from the old fellows of the neighborhood who gathered regularly on the front porch. They crossed their legs, tipped their chairs back, and exchanged tall tales for hours. Johnnie and David called them "store sitters."

The tales were getting taller as the trolley tracks extended closer to Terre Hill.

"Yep," Old George nodded, bobbing up and down, "them are Italians working down there."

"And they live in tarpaper shacks," added Bald Amos. "Makes for cheap labor."

"Those Italians—they speak so that we cannot understand," commented Frank, "and I wouldn't doubt they steal when they have a chance."

"But, but . . ." stuttered Sober Solly, "they work hard with their picks and shovels. Who would do it if they wouldn't?"

Johnnie stepped into the circle and interrupted the conversation. "Have they come as far as our farm yet? You know they bought the right-of-way to do so."

"Yeah, yeah." The men nodded. "Maybe today they'll move right into that lower field."

"They have plenty of horses and wagons going. That Conestoga Traction Company has the equipment to make things happen!" Old George said.

"They are already hauling in metal beams and stuff for that bridge they are building across the Conestoga," Bald Amos added.

"It takes a lot of gravel from the quarry for the road bed," said Sober Solly.

"The steel for the rails gets hauled in by steam train from Pittsburgh," Old George put in.

Johnnie stood quietly, gathering all the information. *Someday I will have to go and see all this for myself,* he thought.

Several more weeks went by and the construction of the trolley line continued to be the talk of the neighborhood. Young and old alike watched the progress, but they kept their distance from the strange Italians.

One Sunday afternoon David buried his nose in the *Martyrs Mirror.* He read aloud to Johnnie until Johnnie got up and stretched. "I'm going for a walk," he said.

David said, "I will stay here and rest. My back always hurts worse after sitting in church all morning."

Johnnie took his cane and walked to the new trolley tracks. The worksite was quiet on a Sunday afternoon. He stooped over, rubbing his hands along the metal rails. *I wonder where the workers go on Sunday,* he thought. *I guess it is no use inviting them to church if they don't know English or German.* Johnnie followed the tracks to the new bridge that spanned the gently-flowing Conestoga Creek. His hands slipped up the sturdy angle irons, and he envisioned the structure as it had been described to him. Groping around, he found crosspieces going up. Placing one foot above the other, he triumphantly climbed higher and higher, testing every piece with his hands and feet. Slowly but surely he went to the top, examining the beams and braces as he went.

He heard voices approaching. Then someone hollered, "Johnnie! How are you going to get down?"

Grinning, he shouted back, "The same way I came up!" He knew it was his uncle Eli and his cousin Clarence. He heard the babble of more people and decided it was time to come down. He was not going to prolong the show.

Eventually the trolley line was completed all the way from Blue Ball to Terre Hill. Now Johnnie could walk down the road and over the bridge past the Weaverland Roller Mills and catch the trolley to go many places. By this time, trolley lines crisscrossed the county like a huge spider web. Johnnie had seen many changes in his day.

|||||||||||||||||||||||||||||||||||||||||||||

One day Johnnie stopped at the store and checked on David, who was busy with customers. He paused on the porch and pricked up his ears when he heard the word *telephone.*

"Yeah," Old George drawled, "Alexander Graham Bell claims he can talk across wires."

"That's not all," interrupted Bald Amos. "There is a line between Boston and Providence. People really are talking back and forth."

"Sure, it won't be long until we see poles and lines all around us," added Frank. He always sat holding his two hands over his big belly, his broad suspenders pulling his trousers up to his armpits. "You are all way behind. Telephones are not so rare in the cities. They will soon be in the country."

Johnnie heard enough to keep his mind churning as he walked to the broom shop behind the store. *I think I need a telephone. Next time I go to Philadelphia I will get the facts. Just think what I could do if I could* talk *to the dealers in Batavia instead of having David write to them. That would be a great asset to our farm equipment business.*

||||||||||||||||||||||||||||||||||||||||||||

Johnnie did not forget his telephone idea. Wechter's Store in Terre Hill had a telephone, and people could now make long distance calls from there. Johnnie wished Mama would have lived to see the day. She would have been so fascinated with the idea. He was not so sure what

Papa would think of him getting a telephone, but he had made the decision and he was going to pursue it. David did not object. In fact, he thought it might eliminate some of Johnnie's town trips and that would be good.

So the arrangements were made. Many neighbors gathered on a fine spring morning in 1907 to watch as the first telephone was installed in their community. The men from the telephone company pulled wires in from the poles beside the road. Some spectators scoffed at the idea and declared it would never work. Others eyed the whole procedure with jealousy. Johnnie excitedly took note of everything the men did, feeling all the equipment and tools and even climbing their ladder. At the end of the day, after the bystanders had dwindled, a telephone was fastened to the wall in the back of Johnnie's store, ready to use.

Johnnie carefully lifted the receiver to his ear and turned the crank on the side of the box. He listened for the operator at the nearest telephone exchange and nervously said, "I would like to speak with Samuel Wechter."

He listened for the *clicks* on the other end and sure enough, he heard Samuel's booming "Hello."

"Hello, this is Johnnie Wenger and I wanted you to know that I have my own phone in our store." He was silent while he listened, and David stood next to him watching every move and listening intently.

"That's right," confirmed Johnnie. "I will let the public use my phone too. Good bye."

Johnnie carefully hung the receiver on the side of the box and clapped his hands in one thunderous clap. "We've got it!" he exclaimed.

But the telephone caused a problem. Soon many neighbors and customers wanted to use the mysterious gadget. Night or day, people arrived to ask for the phone service.

"Johnnie," said David one morning, "I think we made a mistake of installing that telephone in the back room. People are constantly tramping through the store and into those private quarters."

"Hmm," mused Johnnie. "You are right. I am not in the store as much as you are, so I did not realize it."

"What can we do about it?" wondered David. "Don't the lines come into the front room?"

"No, but I can change that. In fact, I will call the company right now!"

After Johnnie hung up the receiver, he informed David, "They say they will come as soon as they can, but they are very busy because so many people are getting new phones."

Johnnie's patience was tried for a month. Then one night as David closed the store he saw Johnnie outside gathering some tools. A ladder rested against the side of the building. *What is my brother up to now?* David wondered. Then it dawned on him, *He is moving that telephone!* When David went to bed that night, he heard thumping and hammering. The ladder scraped against the siding of the house, and David pulled the blanket over his head and prayed. That was the best way he could help his blind brother just now.

Sure enough, the next morning when David met Johnnie

in the store, Johnnie grinned and motioned to the telephone that now hung on the wall right inside the door. The wires came in under the roof just where he wanted them to be.

"Johnnie, what will you do next?" asked David. "I wish Papa could see what you did."

"*Ach,* that's nothing. I just saved some time and expense! Don't forget. It is just as easy for me to work in the night as in the day, and this way I did not disturb the others on the line."

CHAPTER NINE

Needs on Welsh Mountain

"Lydia," Johnnie said one day to his sister, "would you like to go along to the mission on Welsh Mountain next week? Samuel Musselman called me on the telephone and said they have the equipment ready to make brooms. They want me to come and teach the black people how to do it."

The Sunday School Mission was teaching the people on Welsh Mountain better work habits and how to use their money more wisely. As they had opportunity, the missionaries also shared the Gospel with them. This work on Welsh Mountain, about five miles away, was known as the Industrial Mission.[1]

Samuel Musselman was an enthusiastic man who had

---

[1] The Industrial Mission on Welsh Mountain existed from 1889 to 1924.

introduced Bible reading among the young people in the Mennonite Church. He was chosen as director of the Industrial Mission, and he drove up the mountain daily. He hired twenty-two black men to clear land on the mountain and plant crops.

At Johnnie's invitation, Lydia dropped her hand sewing into her lap in disbelief. "Are you really serious?"

"Why, Lydia," asked Johnnie, "when am I not serious?"

They both laughed, knowing that Johnnie was a tease, but he quickly added, "I think it would be good for you. You hardly ever get away from the house, and Barbara can manage by herself for one day. David has to stay here to tend the post office and the store."

"I do feel honored that you ask me," said Lydia. "The strawberry season is nearly over, so I do not need to pick them every day anymore. Really, my work will wait for me. When are you going?"

"Probably next Thursday. We can take the trolley to Blue Ball. Samuel Musselman will be there with his carriage and horse to pick us up. We'll ride up the mountain with him."

Lydia picked up her stitching again, but somehow her fingers could no longer make the fine stitches she had been making, *"Ach,"* she said to Barbara, "why am I so excited?"

She watched Johnnie go out the door and get the bucket to feed his chickens. *Johnnie is such a thoughtful and considerate older brother,* she thought. *I know he sacrifices much for those people on Welsh Mountain.*

On a beautiful June morning, Johnnie and Lydia left for Welsh Mountain. Stepping carefully into the trolley, Lydia found an empty seat close to the front. Cool breezes floated in through the open window. She tied her bonnet securely under her chin and tucked her long skirts around her legs to make room for other passengers. Johnnie slipped into the seat on the opposite side. "The trolley is so empty this morning," he commented.

"Oh, the fields are such a pretty green," Lydia described as the trolley moved along. "So many trees are in full bloom. I see a farmer cultivating the tiny tobacco plants. A woman is in a lovely garden scratching with her hoe. A young girl with her bonnet dangling down her back is picking strawberries. I wonder if she is still finding many."

It was natural for Lydia to be eyes for Johnnie while they traveled. Together they enjoyed the sunny morning. Johnnie sniffed the fragrant air and exclaimed, "I smell lilacs along the tracks! And farther back I could tell a farmer was hauling manure out to the field. I heard he had one of those wonderful manure spreaders.

"Lydia, do you know what to expect today?" wondered Johnnie, changing the subject. "You know the mountain people still live in log cabins, and sometimes many people live in one shack. Children dressed in rags share the yards with pigs and chickens."

"Yes, Hannah told me on Sunday they are a bunch of thieves, and she would not go up there."

"Oh, there is nothing to worry about," said Johnnie. "The Mennonites have done much to help the people with

Sunday schools and church services. And now they have this mission."

"Hannah says they do bone hauling and pick huckleberries to make a living," Lydia said.

"Yes, they come to the market at Lancaster," Johnnie said. "Someone described their wagons as made with the shreds and patches from a wagon maker's shop. No two wheels are alike. The wagon wobbles and the horses are often blind or lame or both. The harness is made out of bits and pieces from a saddle shop. Bits of rope tie it all together."

Lydia inhaled sharply in disbelief, but Johnnie continued. "You know, it is a pity, because these people cannot really help their situation. Some are Indian, and others are white. Many are the descendants of black slaves who lost their income from charcoal making when coal mining started. And some came to the mountain after the Fugitive Slave Law was passed."

"And what was the Fugitive Slave Law?"

"Lydia, are you ready for a history lesson?" Johnnie grinned and shifted in his seat.

"The Fugitive Slave Law imposed heavy penalties upon anyone who helped a slave escape. The law was revived and strengthened in 1850. That was when I was seven years old and before you were born," Johnnie added. "In my day, right here in Lancaster County, many slaves who had escaped from the South found refuge in barns and cellars. Some fled to the mountains like scared rabbits. They had absolutely nothing—nothing more than they could carry on their backs."

Johnnie turned his face heavenward as he often did when he was thinking deeply. *Just think how different the history is for us Mennonites whose ancestors came across the sea. And now we come together—the descendants of the slaves from Africa and the Mennonites from Europe— meeting on Welsh Mountain.*

Turning to Lydia he added, "Surely we have something to offer these poor people, and more than just potatoes!"

Lydia laughed. "You must have heard what Deacon Ike Hershey said, 'Poor people in the community need our prayers. Prayers are good, but prayers and potatoes are better!'

"Oh, here we are, already in Blue Ball! That was a short ride," said Lydia as she prepared to step out of the trolley.

Samuel Musselman waved to them from the carriage where he was waiting at the hitching rail. "Good morning," he greeted Johnnie and Lydia and shook hands heartily. "Johnnie, I am so glad you brought your sister along today. My wife would also have liked to come along, but it is best if she stays at home with the children.

"Lydia, you just hop on the back seat there. And don't be surprised if I find another passenger to sit beside you. Usually I find someone along the way who needs a ride up the mountain."

I hope it is a woman, thought Lydia as she climbed gracefully into the carriage.

Johnnie and Samuel were soon engaged in a serious conversation. Lydia absorbed the beauty of the ride up the mountain as she clung to the edge of the seat. After

several minutes, trees enveloped them and the narrow road became even narrower. The carriage rattled over rocks and large twigs, and sometimes they swerved around bigger branches. Openings among the trees were like windows framed by lacy leaf curtains, and Lydia got a view of the patchwork of farmland spread over Lancaster County and the Pequea Valley. Captivated by the breathtaking view, she did not notice the old lady ahead of them with a huge market basket hanging on her arm. Samuel pulled in the reins and hollered in a friendly way, "Good day, Rose! Do you want a ride up to your cabin?"

"Sure, sure," responded Rose without hesitation. Clambering into the back of the carriage, she plopped down beside Lydia. Her black face was fringed with black curly hair that stuck out like sheep's wool from her grimy red bandana. Lydia noticed a mess of berries in the bottom of the market basket balanced on Rose's feet. On top of the berries lay a handful of wild garlic. Not knowing how to respond to the woman's perpetual, white-toothed grin, Lydia just smiled. She tried not to stare at Rose's skirt, which clung to her like a wet rag. Her sweater hung over her shoulders, hiding a blouse that had left its traces of lace behind.

"Where you going?" asked Rose, turning her face to look squarely at Lydia. "Are you visitin' Betsy?"

Lydia squirmed and nodded a friendly yes, still wondering how to act like a missionary.

"Who's dat?" asked Rose pointing a finger at Johnnie.

"That is my brother. His name is John. He will help make brooms."

"Aha," nodded Rose. "He ben here afore. He's funny. He's blind as a bat."

Lydia was not sure what to think of all her comments, but just then Johnnie turned around and said, "How is Elmer?"

"Oooh, he fine, fine. He said he dreams about brooms. He fly away with 'em!" Then she roared with laughter, and the rest chuckled because there was nothing funnier than Rose herself.

Approaching the end of the journey, they came to the top of the mountain where two roads intersected at a place called *Hand Boards.* Samuel pulled his horse to a halt for a rest. Like Moses on Mount Pisgah, Lydia gazed in wonder at the magnificent view of rural prosperity. Villages and farm buildings, cultivated fields and groves, hills and valleys stretched out below her as far as the eye could see.

"Johnnie," she exclaimed, "with one sweep of my eyes, I can see more of Lancaster County than I ever did before!"

Johnnie smiled, absorbing the fresh mountain air, smelling the woodsy aroma of the pines, and listening to the birds. He turned his eyes toward the sky and said, "I am so glad I can be here! I enjoy this mountain as much as anybody could."

"Now we shall go to the mission over here," said Samuel, guiding his horse to the east. "This is where we have cleared land and planted crops and fruit trees. And over there is Noah Mack's stone house. He is probably in school already this morning. " He pointed a finger that Johnnie could not see, but Johnnie nodded in agreement.

"Here is the broomcorn already sprouting! Good! We hope to grow enough so the people can make brooms and earn a profit. We had to buy some broomcorn last winter, and there is still plenty here for you to work with today," said Samuel as he started unhitching his horse in front of the two-story building known as the Industrial Mission.

Noah Mack's wife Betsy shook Lydia's hand heartily. "I am so glad to see you came along! I do like to see sisters from Weaverland during the week sometimes."

Lydia glanced over her shoulder as she followed Betsy. Johnnie was already surrounded by excited "colored folks," the term black people used to describe themselves. They were ready to hear and see more of this "broom maker," as they called Johnnie.

"Why don't I show you around here a bit before we go over to my house and peel potatoes?" suggested Betsy. They walked up the steps to the upper part of the building. Here Lydia watched Lydia Stauffer, the supervisor in the shirt factory, directing the sewing project. She greeted the visitors with a smile as she explained to a fidgety young lady how to carefully cut around the pattern laid on the shirt material. Taking some pins from her mouth, she pinned the pattern securely to the material before she handed the scissors to the eager black girl.

"Yep, I can do it!" the girl exclaimed as she twirled the scissors before getting down to business.

Then Lydia Stauffer stepped over to an elderly lady with kinky hair tied in a knot on the back of her head. "Do you have a problem?" The lady hunched over her sewing machine and tried desperately to get the thread through the eye of the needle. "I cannot see dat needle eye! My sight so bad!"

"Let me help you," said Lydia kindly, as she bent and slipped the thread through the eye. "Did you know the blind man came to help Elmer Boots make brooms today?" she asked.

The elderly lady sat up straight and exclaimed, "Dat is good! I want to see him too."

"You will see him at lunchtime," Lydia said as more eyes turned her way.

The sewing machines hummed along. Above the purr of the machines, they heard the constant *putt-putt-putt* of the gasoline engines that powered the machines.

"I will show you the downstairs yet before we go over to my house," said Betsy.

Lydia followed through the dim stairwell. She heard much talking and laughing, then she saw her brother. There he was, patiently laying out the broomcorn just as he did at home. Carefully explaining how to grab a bunch, and with the wire tension just right, he wrapped it around the handle. A broom took shape as his deft hands skillfully handled the tools. Lydia wished Johnnie could see those who were watching. Their shiny eyes glistened in the dim lighting and their grins showed pleasure.

Lydia heard Johnnie say, "Yes, yes, I've been making brooms for almost forty years—I have probably made thousands!

"No, Elmer, you must not trim it too much. It sweeps

better if you keep the ends softer." Lydia could have stayed and watched Johnnie longer, but Betsy was ready to show her the carpet looms.

"Today nobody is weaving," Betsy explained. "You know we make those rag rugs, but the hard part is getting enough material for rags. These mountain folks *wear* their rags and do not throw anything away, so much of the stuff we weave comes from the valley."

Now that is something I could contribute to the mission, Lydia thought as she walked along. *I am sure I could help collect some material.*

Her thoughts were interrupted when she heard sweet singing float from the upstairs where the women were sewing. "Do they often sing as they work?" she wondered.

"Oh, yes," said Betsy, walking toward the house. "This place rings with many Gospel songs!"

While visiting, the ladies deftly peeled potatoes and tossed them into the bubbling kettle of soup on the old cook stove. As they prepared dinner, Lydia learned much about the mission. Betsy told her about the poverty among the mountain people and the thieving raids by the gang known as the Buzzards. But she also spoke of the efforts put into Sunday schools, the church services conducted by the Mennonites, and how this Industrial Mission provided work and income for many. She praised Johnnie for the effort he put into the work and told Lydia how Elmer Boots certainly had changed his ways for the better.

At lunch time Lydia grabbed one handle of the pot and Betsy the other. Together they lugged the kettle of soup to the table in the shirt factory. They filled baskets with fresh bread and opened several jars of pickles. Betsy pulled a crumb cake from the oven and directed Lydia to get a pitcher full of milk from the can in the springhouse. When the ladies had the dinner ready, Samuel rang a bell and everyone gathered around the table. Lydia listened to the bits and pieces of conversation and enjoyed the interaction immensely.

"Johnnie, do you have one of those telephones in your store?"

"I heard of a man who made a machine they call a horseless carriage!"

"Naw! That's not possible!"

"Did you know Abe Buzzard is in jail again?"

"Can't be. I heard him preach and he is awful sorry he stole!"

"Well," said Samuel Musselman gravely, "I am sorry, but Abe Buzzard seems to be a hypocrite. He preaches while his gang is out stealing, and I am afraid you are right; he is in jail again."

Lydia, noticing a sad-looking woman wipe tears from her eyes, wondered what her connection might be with the gang. She was glad to hear the subject change to crops, weather, school, church, and other ordinary things.

Early in the afternoon Samuel came to the house to tell Lydia it was time to ride down the mountain again.

Lydia watched Elmer Boots vigorously shake Johnnie's hand before he climbed into the carriage to leave. Elmer thanked Johnnie profusely for coming and helping the mountain people make brooms.

"God bless you!" said Johnnie as he waved goodbye. Slowly the carriage wheels turned toward Blue Ball again.

Lydia and Johnnie had much to talk about as the trolley rolled toward Weaverland. "I see we have so much to be thankful for!" exclaimed Johnnie. "We had such good parents who took us to church and taught us how to work and how to live a godly life. Just think of all the opportunities we have because of where we were born. What if you and I would be mountain people, or what if our forefathers would have been slaves from Africa who had not met Jesus yet? I see such a need for more teaching—oh, I wish I could do more for them!"

"Thank you for taking me along today," said Lydia as she stepped from the trolley. "I learned so much about the mountain people. I see a need I never realized existed before. Let's do what we can!"

CHAPTER TEN

Changes

"David, listen to this. I am so amazed!" Johnnie could not conceal his enthusiasm. "Silas Gehman got his buggy running."

"You mean the one with an engine?"

"Yep! He went all the way to the Mennonite community in Spring City! Imagine what that looked like. No horse. An engine puttering along, and there Silas sat with a lever in his hand to guide the rig."

"Did he ever get that steam engine running?" wondered David.

"Oh yes, he has several going. Peter Shirk is working on a horseless carriage too. I hope I get to ride in it. I never thought I would see the day!"

"I imagine a machine like that would be enough to scare any horse and send him into the ditch."

The two brothers were walking along on their way home from Weaverland Mennonite Church, discussing tidbits of news they heard after the sermon.

"Wasn't that a wonderful English sermon?" said David. "Amos Herr would have been impressed to hear us sing his song in church this morning."

"Well, it is true; we do owe the Lord a morning song! I wonder what he all had in mind when he wrote that song," mused Johnnie.

"I wonder what J. Weaver would have to say if he would know how often we have evening services now?"

"Remember when he came all the way from Kansas with his horse and wagon to preach for us, and we had an evening service?" asked Johnnie. "Papa was still here to see that happen. Remember how we helped put up brackets along the wall to hold the lamps?"

"Didn't some lamps hang from the ceiling?"

"David, don't forget that the lights made no difference to me! But I do remember the novelty of the first evening service."

"I wonder what Papa would say about all these horse-less carriages."

"He would be all for it!" said Johnnie. "He liked new things. I wish he could see how many things we can do with electricity in our day."

The discussion came to an end as the brothers walked across the porch and into the farmhouse. Barbara and

Lydia had the table spread, and the aroma of a Sunday dinner greeted Johnnie and David as well as many other guests who came to spend the day with them.

In the afternoon a circle of men sat on chairs under the shade trees in the lawn. Johnnie enjoyed these times. He was a good entertainer and his friends loved to hear the tales of his travels. He told them about his recent trip to Washington County, Maryland, to visit relatives. He talked about train trips he had taken to Virginia, Ohio, and Indiana.

Old Hans rose from his chair and stretched. "Johnnie, you 'see' more of the world than the rest of us do!"

"Ach," said Pete, pushing his chair back. "It must be about time to go home and milk. These evening services make Sunday afternoons shorter."

"Johnnie, what time is it?" wondered Sober Solly. He loved to ask that question because he wanted Johnnie to pull out his pocket watch and show it to those around him.

Slowly Johnnie's hand slipped into his pocket. Everyone was quiet as all eyes turned to the rare timepiece that Johnnie plucked out. He pushed the little knob beside the stem, and they all listened as the watch struck four, then four more strikes in a different tone, to indicate that it was quarter after four. Next they heard five softer strikes which meant it was five minutes past four fifteen, indicating the time was twenty minutes after four.

Shaking their heads in amazement, curious guests crowded around Johnnie. "And where did you find that?" wondered George.

"I found it in Philadelphia."

"I suppose you paid a pretty price!"

"To tell you the truth," offered Johnnie, "I had to pay one hundred dollars for it."

"Oh. Oh!" A little ripple of amazement flowed through the crowd. But they knew the blind man deserved it.

After hitching up their horses, the guests left for home.

David followed Johnnie to his room. He sat down and pulled a chair close to Johnnie. "Do you want me to read to you?" This was a common thing for David to do. For many years, he had read aloud to Johnnie—the Bible, the newspapers, the *Herald of Truth*, and now the Sunday school quarterlies.

"No," answered Johnnie, smiling. "I think I can handle it by myself this afternoon. I have mastered reading those raised letters with my fingers. That school for the blind in Philadelphia has helped me so much. I sure appreciated the chart they gave me with the Lord's Prayer in raised letters. But David, I could never have mastered reading without your help."

"It's amazing," agreed David. "I love watching you read by yourself. But if you would not have been determined and patient at the same time, I never could have taught you."

Picking up the bulky copy of the Gospel of Mark, Johnnie brushed his fingers carefully over the raised letters. "Thank you, David. You have done so much for me. Being able to read is another blessing straight from the Lord! I am so happy that I can read some by myself. You are free to read books to yourself this afternoon."

David slowly rose to his feet, ready to leave Johnnie

alone. Abruptly Johnnie stopped moving his fingers and said, "David, did you know that this week I am going with Martin Weaver to see the old Hans Herr house?"

David stopped in his tracks. "Johnnie, I am so glad you get that opportunity. I know you always wanted to do that. Isn't that the oldest house in Lancaster County?"

Johnnie replied, "Yes." David could see that Johnnie was not into discussing history just now. He watched Johnnie's fingers glide over the page. Stepping softly from the room, David closed the door behind him. *I am so glad Johnnie had the perseverance to learn reading on his own in his old age. He has always been able to take care of himself, but this adds a new dimension to his life.*

Johnnie, enjoying the Scriptures like he always did, read page after page. He loved the chapter in Mark 8 that included the story of the blind man who received his sight. *What would I do if Jesus walked on the earth* today? *But really, God is so good to me. And seeing God working in my life and saving me is more important than physical sight. I can walk with God today and someday—in that unclouded day—I shall see Him! When the mists have rolled away . . .*

Later in the week, Martin Weaver came to the door of Johnnie's house all set to travel to the Pequea settlement to see the historical Hans Herr house. They decided to travel by trolley as far as they could even if it meant walking some at the other end of the trip.

In the graveyard near the Hans Herr house, Johnnie knelt and read the old grave markers with his fingers. He shook his head as he tried to comprehend what it was like

two hundred years earlier when the first Mennonites settled into that area. "Just think of it," he said, "some of these people came across the ocean from Germany or Switzerland to preserve the faith we still hold and practice today."

Martin showed him the way into the old sandstone house built by Christian Herr in 1719. It was empty and smelled like an old cellar. Johnnie tried to picture the time when this building was used as a dwelling and a meeting house. "Just imagine what it looked like when the Indians crowded in here on a cold winter evening or when they set up benches for a church service. I can just imagine the slow singing and Hans Burkholder's German preaching!" He started feeling along the walls, as if history would be written there. "This house," he said, "was built like the houses they had in Switzerland."

"Yes," agreed Martin, "but at the same time some Mennonites were building log cabins. Not everyone built a solid 'mansion' like this!"

"The Mennonites were prosperous farmers and landowners at that time already," said Johnnie thoughtfully. As he made his way around the empty house, his hands glided over the stone lintels, the woodwork, wooden pins and door hinges, the fireplace, and the oak floors. They spoke volumes to the blind man. Martin, with his hands in his pockets, stood back and watched as Johnnie's fingers carefully traced the date and initials carved above the door—17CHHR19.

For a long time his hands moved over the fascinating

stair steps hewn from solid logs. One quarter of each log was hewn out. These logs were pinned together with wooden beams going up the side of the staircase.

After Johnnie was satisfied that he had "seen" everything, they started on their journey home.

Johnnie and Martin discussed history all the way home. "Just think of it. Lancaster County wasn't even formed when the Swiss emigrants received the grant for ten thousand acres of land."

"That's right. Lancaster County was formed on May 10, 1729," said Martin.

"Hans Herr was their first preacher, wasn't he?"

"Yes. And Christian was his son," affirmed Martin.

"I have heard that the fertile fields along the Pequea Creek attracted the Swiss-German families because they resembled the farmland of Palatinate, Germany."

"The Swiss Mennonites had emigrated from Switzerland to Germany, and from there they moved to Holland and England because of persecution," said Martin.

"We cannot imagine what they had to go through before they came to America," marveled Johnnie.

"Trading with the Indians would have been a new experience too," Martin pointed out.

"I know the Pequea Trading Post was just south of Lancaster."

"They could never have imagined traveling on the roads we do today or gliding along rails in a trolley," said Johnnie. "They followed Indian trails."

"Yes," agreed Martin, "but it is amazing how soon they

had better roads and had their farms established. Just think of what we see now almost two hundred years later."

"And so many meeting places have been established in so many districts," Johnnie observed.

"We cannot imagine what it will be like in another one hundred years from now!"

"History will always be in the making."

"Thank you for taking me to visit the Hans Herr house," Johnnie said when they finally returned to Weaverland. "It is a real historical landmark."

A new year came and with it the full blast of winter. David watched Johnnie as he sat by the little potbellied stove in the store. "What are you doing now?" wondered David, moving closer. On the floor was a pile of shavings that had dropped from the knife in Johnnie's hands. He turned the piece of wood and held it up for David to see. David looked puzzled. "And what is it?" he asked.

"When I am finished you will know," said Johnnie with a grin. His knife kept carving away until a replica of a stairway emerged in the palm of his hand.

"Look here," he called to David at the other end of the store. "Do you remember what I told you about the stairs in the Hans Herr house?" David stepped to Johnnie's side and gazed at the model, and then at Johnnie, in silent amazement. This blind brother of his had accomplished so much in his lifetime.

Johnnie reached for the broom and swept up the shavings. Bit by bit he tossed them into the blazing fire, enjoying the crackling outbursts of flame. The wind howled around the building just as it had long ago when the family lived together in East Earl Township. "David," he mused, "I've seen so much in my lifetime. Remember going to Jeremiah's shop in Goodwill with me when I wanted to learn how to make brooms?"

David pulled a chair up to the fire and slowly eased himself into it. "Yes, and who would have ever imagined how big the business would get. Those brooms swept us off our feet!"

Johnnie smiled fondly. "Remember moving day? The first little store we had?"

"Then we added the post office and built the implement shed," recalled David.

"I can't believe we managed to get the telephone as soon as we did. Now we wouldn't know what to do without it!"

The brothers reminisced until darkness enveloped them and the only light in the shop was the reflection of the flickering flames in the stove, dancing on the wall and ceiling.

Indeed, Johnnie had seen many opportunities in his lifetime.[1] He had been able to do good, to help others, and to build the church. He had encouraged many lives in his home, in his business, in the church, and in his travels. God had blessed him with courage to rise above his blindness. Johnnie looked forward to the glorious day when he would at last *see* his Savior and King.

---

[1] "Blind Johnnie," John S. Wenger, lived from 1843 to 1916.

About the Author

Velina Showalter was born in 1952 and raised in an Old Order Mennonite home in Ontario, Canada. She taught school for twenty years, the last seven of which were in Farmington, New Mexico. In 1989 she married John Showalter, a widower who had five children. Three more children were added to the family by this union. In 1993 the family moved to Grand Junction, Colorado, where they lived for ten years before moving to their current residence near Greencastle, Pennsylvania. Velina and her husband are members of the Paradise Mennonite Church in Washington County, Maryland.

Velina loves the Lord and the work of His kingdom. Writing is her hobby and a way to bless others. She is the author of *Amanda Musselman, Four Angels, Blind Martha, Nobody's Boy,* and the full-color version of *Blind Johnnie,* all published by CAM.

Researching to write biographies has given her enjoyable interviews with source persons and rewarding times in historical libraries. Children as well as adults can benefit from Velina's efforts to bring to life outstanding persons in our Anabaptist heritage.

You can contact Velina by writing to her in care of Christian Aid Ministries, P.O. Box 360, Berlin, Ohio 44610.

About Christian Aid Ministries

Christian Aid Ministries was founded in 1981 as a non-profit, tax-exempt 501(c)(3) organization. Its primary purpose is to provide a trustworthy and efficient channel for Amish, Mennonite, and other conservative Anabaptist groups and individuals to minister to physical and spiritual needs around the world. This is in response to the command to ". . . do good unto all men, especially unto them who are of the household of faith" (Galatians 6:10).

Each year, CAM supporters provide 15–20 million pounds of food, clothing, medicines, seeds, Bibles, Bible story books, and other Christian literature for needy people. Most of the aid goes to orphans and Christian families. Supporters' funds also help to clean up and rebuild for natural disaster victims, put up Gospel billboards in the U.S., support several church-planting efforts, operate two medical clinics, and provide resources for needy families to make their own living. CAM's main purposes for providing aid are to help and encourage God's people and bring the Gospel to a lost and dying world.

CAM has staff, warehouses, and distribution networks in Romania, Moldova, Ukraine, Haiti, Nicaragua, Liberia, Israel, and Kenya. Aside from management, supervisory personnel, and bookkeeping operations, volunteers do most of the work at CAM locations. Each year, volunteers at our warehouses, field bases, Disaster Response Services projects, and other locations donate over 200,000 hours of work.

CAM's ultimate purpose is to glorify God and help enlarge His kingdom. ". . . whatsoever ye do, do all to the glory of God" (1 Corinthians 10:31).